A Fragile Foundation

The State of Developmental Assets among American Youth

Peter L. Benson, Peter C. Scales, Nancy Leffert, and
Eugene C. Roehlkepartain

Search
INSTITUTE

The resource is part of Search Institute's Healthy Communities •
Healthy Youth initiative, which seeks to unite individuals, organizations,
and communities for children and adolescents. Major corporate support
for this initiative is provided by Lutheran Brotherhood, a member-owned
organization of more than 1 million Lutherans joined together for financial security, benevolent outreach, and volunteer service. Lutheran
Brotherhood demonstrates its stewardship through programs that
strengthen communities and serve Lutheran congregations and
institutions.

A Fragile Foundation:
The State of Developmental Assets among American Youth
By Peter L. Benson, Peter C. Scales, Nancy Leffert, and Eugene C. Roehlkepartain
Copyright © 1999 by Search Institute

10   9   8   7   6   5   4   3   2

Printed in the United States of America on acid-free paper.

Library of Congress Cataloging-in-Publication Data

    A fragile foundation : the state of developmental assets among
American youth / Peter L. Benson . . . [et al.].
      p.   cm.
    Includes bibliographical references.
    ISBN 1-57482-352-3 (acid-free paper)
    1. Child development—Research—United States. 2. Adolescent
psychology—Research—United States. 3. Children—Research—United
States. I. Benson, Peter L.
    HQ767.85.F73   1999
    305.231—dc21   99–12993

Search Institute
700 South Third Street, Suite 210
Minneapolis, MN 55415
612-376-8955
800-888-7828
www.search-institute.org

Credits
Editing:	Kathryn (Kay) L. Hong
Design and Illustration:	Wendy J. Johnson, Points Of View, Inc.
Cover photography:	Joel Grimes Photography, courtesy of Assets for Colorado Youth, Denver

Contents

Contents

Shared Challenges, Shared Opportunities

In recent years, the United States has engaged in much collective hand-wringing about problems and challenges facing young people. One opinion poll after another shows that youth-related issues top people's lists of concerns and priorities. People consistently ask politicians and other leaders to improve education; reduce youth violence; prevent young people from using alcohol, tobacco, or other drugs; or declare "war" on some other youth-related problem.

While most people agree that something has gone wrong, there is much less agreement about how to make more things go right. Yet a growing number of experts and leaders in youth development, education, prevention, juvenile justice, public health, and other fields are calling for a new focus on building a solid foundation that can help young people cope and thrive.

This report, *A Fragile Foundation: The State of Developmental Assets among American Youth,* presents both a framework for understanding positive factors that contribute to healthy development—which we call "developmental assets"—and a portrait of 6th- to 12th-grade youth based on that framework.

At least three important themes recur throughout this report:

1. *All young people are affected.* The foundation for healthy development is too fragile for virtually all young people, regardless of their background and circumstances.

2. The real story lies not in the details of individual assets, high-risk behaviors, deficits, or thriving indicators. Rather, *the power lies in putting all these pieces together to bring positive and protective aspects into the lives of all young people.*

3. *Everyone plays a role,* both in contributing to the current situation and in taking action to strengthen the foundation for the future.

Theme #1: All Young People Are Affected

The challenges and opportunities identified in this report speak to all types of youth, all types of communities, all types of families. In terms of developmental assets, no group of youth is far better off or far worse off than other groups. No group is immune; no group is cursed. All young people—including those who "have everything" and those who have little—need society to pay more attention to their care and nurture.

When we examine young people's experiences of developmental assets (Chapter 2), we see that too many young people do not experience these positive relationships and opportunities, leaving them with a fragile foundation upon which to build their lives. On the average, the 99,462 surveyed adolescents report experiencing only 18 of the 40 developmental assets. Almost two-thirds of the young people surveyed possess half or fewer of the 40 assets.

In addition to the lack of assets for most youth, we see that deficits and patterns of high-risk behavior are widespread among these middle and high school youth. (See Chapter 3.) The average young person surveyed experiences 1.9 of the 5 deficits measured. Furthermore, almost half of the young people surveyed (47 percent) report being involved in 2 or more of the 10 dangerous patterns of high-risk behavior that are studied.

To be sure, some important differences exist among various subgroups of youth (i.e., grade, gender, race/ethnicity, family composition, level of mother's education, and type of community). These differences are presented in the report and the appendixes, and they need further investigation and focused attention. But most striking are the commonalities across all the groups of young people surveyed.

Theme #2: The Power Lies in Adding Together All the Pieces

One wouldn't necessarily reach the conclusion that virtually all young people are building their lives on a fragile foundation by looking just at isolated areas of their lives. Nor would you notice the power of many assets if you focused on just a few of them. The power and impact become evident as you put all the pieces together in a mosaic of young people's lives, and then step back and look at the big picture.

For example, each of the individual patterns of high-risk behavior is experienced by between 18 and 33 percent of young people. We might pick any one of these behaviors (e.g., violence) and say that targeted prevention or intervention efforts could be effective in addressing that problem. However, the challenge comes when we find that only one-third of young people report none of these patterns of high-risk behavior.

When all the pieces are drawn together, we see that only 4 percent of young people report having all of the following elements:

- 31 or more of the 40 assets;

- 1 or none of the 5 deficits;

- 2 or fewer of the 10 high-risk behavior patterns; and

- at least 6 of the 8 thriving indicators.

Thus, the vast majority of young people are building their lives on a foundation that truly is fragile. Some—perhaps most—young people will still manage to navigate through adolescence into adulthood relatively unscathed, despite their circumstances and some of the harmful choices they make. Too many will not, however. For them, experiences in their early years will leave scars that will take years to heal, if they heal at all. And some will become trapped in negative cycles of violence, addiction, and hopelessness that will deprive both themselves and their community of their potential and contribution.

But this is not the end of the story. The mosaic of young people's lives has a hopeful theme. That hope becomes evident in the potential that developmental assets have to shape young people's choices. As shown in Chapter 4, young people who experience the most developmental assets are least likely to engage in problem behaviors and most likely to thrive. Intentionally working to ensure that more young people experience many of the assets offers a positive, hopeful path to a brighter future for young people and society.

Theme #3: Everyone Plays a Role

Too often, reports on young people focus attention on specific gaps in their lives, laying blame for the problems on a particular institution or segment of society. Some Americans point to parents as the primary culprits behind problems facing young people. Others blame schools or the public sector for inadequately preparing young people for life.

The data based on the framework of developmental assets make it difficult to lay blame on any single institution or group of people. Indeed, all elements of society share both the blame and the responsibility for many of the challenges facing young people. For example, one of the most striking statistics in the framework of developmental assets is that only about one in five young people say they experience asset #7: community values youth.

There is plenty of blame to go around. But more important is the critical need to shift away from pointing fingers to joining hands. The framework of developmental assets offers common ground where all segments of communities can explore together how everyone can support and encourage our young people in their growth and positive development.

By focusing attention on ensuring that all young people experience the developmental assets, individuals, families, organizations, and communities can begin to transform a fragile foundation into a solid foundation for life. But it will take all of us—parents, peers, neighbors, teachers, leaders, businesses, volunteers, and others—recognizing our own potential for contributing to the health and well-being of all young people.

Overview of This Report

This report provides the first extensive portrait of American youth based on data from a survey—*Search Institute Profiles of Student Life: Attitudes and Behaviors*—that measures 40 developmental assets. It analyzes and interprets data collected from 99,462 youth in 213 communities during the 1996–97 school year. It is organized as follows:

- Chapter 1 gives the background about assets and the young people surveyed.

- Chapter 2 focuses on young people's experiences of developmental assets, offering in-depth information about each of the eight categories of assets.

- Chapter 3 shifts to examine the deficits and patterns of high-risk behavior that threaten to compromise young people's healthy development.

- Chapter 4 builds links between the developmental assets and the deficits and risky behaviors, showing the power that assets have in reducing young people's involvement in high-risk behaviors and in mitigating the negative effect of deficits. In addition, this chapter shows how assets promote eight thriving indicators.

- Chapter 5 pulls the pieces together, suggesting an overall goal for well-being that takes into account the assets, deficits, patterns of high-risk behavior, and thriving indicators. It then high-lights a series of creative tensions that must be kept in mind in addressing the challenges and opportunities that the report presents.

Each chapter includes text, figures, and tables that offer details about patterns and differences that emerge from the data. Throughout the text are tables that show data by grade and gender—the two demographic areas where differences consistently appear. The appendixes offer additional details related to other demographic differences: race/ethnicity, type of community, family composition, and maternal education.

Fueling a Movement

This report focuses on documenting the realities in young people's lives. In doing so, we hope it fuels a national movement to shore up the foundation that all young people need to ensure that they are—and become—caring, contributing, and resourceful members of families, communities, and society.

That movement is already under way. At the time of this writing, more than 300 communities have begun initiatives designed to unite, motivate, and equip all sectors of the community to work together to build assets for youth. In addition, dozens of national and regional organizations and thousands of individuals are exploring their own capacity and opportunities for asset building.

Acknowledgments

The information that is distilled into these pages grows out of the commitments, efforts, and contributions from many people and places.

No organization has been more pivotal in the survey process that undergirds this report than Lutheran Brotherhood, a member-owned financial services organization. Without Lutheran Brotherhood's support for and commitment to strengthening communities, much of Search Institute's asset-building work in the past decade would not have been possible.

Lutheran Brotherhood commissioned Search Institute to create the original survey that measured 30 assets in 1989 and has continued to be a major partner in this effort, including funding for *The Troubled Journey,* the precursor to this report. In addition, Lutheran Brotherhood has subsidized the cost of conducting the survey in hundreds of communities, including those represented in this report. We particularly thank Louise Thoreson and Ellen Albee, who have become our colleagues and friends through this partnership.

Another vital link in this process is the involvement of communities in gathering data. Though each community conducted the survey to learn about its own youth, the aggregate sample in this report gives us insight into the larger context. Thanks to the participating communities for being part of the picture.

We also want to thank the many colleagues at Search Institute who have contributed to this report. The survey services department—Dyanne Drake, Jean Wachs, and Debbie Grillo—was instrumental in working with communities to conduct the surveys. Marilyn Erickson contributed her word processing skills. And our data services colleagues—Tamra Boyce, Karen Pladsen, and Rick Trierweiler—provided endless data analysis and huge stacks of printouts that form the foundation for this report.

Thanks as well to the publishing team that helped refine and polish this manuscript. Special thanks to Kay Hong, whose meticulous attention to detail, eye for what's missing, and commitment to getting it right strengthened the report in innumerable ways. Renee Vraa, Pat Johnson, Karen Pladsen, Kalisha Davis, and Amanda Seigel helped to create tables and charts and double-checked thousands of percentages, facts, and figures to ensure that this report is as accurate as possible. Becky Manfredini, Wendy Johnson, and Mary Byers shepherded the report through design, copyediting, proofreading, and production.

Finally, we thank the reviewers whose insights and comments strengthened this report: Craig Deville, Tom Griffin, and numerous Search Institute colleagues.

A Fragile Foundation: The State of Developmental Assets among American Youth

The United States has engaged in much collective hand-wringing about problems and challenges facing its children and youth. But while most people agree that something has gone wrong in how this society raises its young people, there is much less agreement about how to make more things go right. This report presents both a framework for charting the factors that contribute to healthy development—which we call "developmental assets"—and a portrait of 6th- to 12th-grade youth based on this framework.

Building a Solid Foundation for Healthy Development

To understand the challenges before us and explore the opportunities we have to build a solid foundation for young people's development, this report proposes benchmarks for four elements of young people's well-being:

- having 31 or more of the 40 developmental assets;

- experiencing only 1 or none of the 5 developmental deficits;

- engaging in only 2 or fewer of the 10 high-risk behavior patterns; and

- having at least 6 of the 8 thriving indicators.

When we examine young people's lives in light of these benchmarks, our challenge is clear. Less than 4 percent of youth report experiencing this level of overall well-being. Thus, virtually all young people must try to build their lives on a fragile foundation that not only jeopardizes their future but limits their potential. This report examines each of these elements of well-being in more detail.

Identifying and Measuring Developmental Assets

Undergirding this study is Search Institute's framework of 40 developmental assets. This framework seeks to identify and measure the elements of a strength-based approach to child and adolescent development, grounded in extensive research in adolescent development, prevention, risk reduction, and resiliency. The asset framework offers a set of factors for healthy development that help to increase positive outcomes and protect youth against high-risk behavior.

The assets are both external (provided by families, individuals, and communities) and internal (personal qualities or characteristics of young people). They are grouped into eight categories:

External Assets	Internal Assets
1. Support	5. Commitment to Learning
2. Empowerment	
3. Boundaries and Expectations	6. Positive Values
	7. Social Competencies
4. Constructive Use of Time	8. Positive Identity

Search Institute has measured these assets through surveys of young people in hundreds of communities across the United States. This report is based on the responses of 99,462 6th- to 12th-grade youth in 213 communities who completed the *Profiles of Student Life: Attitudes and Behaviors* survey during the 1996–97 school year. While the sample is not nationally representative, it is large and somewhat diverse, giving a sense of how youth in a significant number of communities describe their lives.

Young People's Experiences of Developmental Assets

Survey responses indicate that the average young person experiences only 18 of the 40 assets. Furthermore, 64 percent of youth report experiencing 20 or fewer of the assets, and 27 of the assets are experienced by half or less of the young people surveyed (Figure 1).

While there is some variability across communities and in different subgroups of youth, the central message is consistent: The vast majority of youth—regardless of age, gender, race/ethnicity, family composition, family income level, or community size—experience far too few of the 40 assets. In short, the very foundation upon which young people must build their lives is fragile for all groups of youth—and all youth could benefit from having more assets.

When we look at young people's experiences of the individual assets, we find that some assets are much more common than others. The assets young people are most likely to report experiencing include:

- Positive view of personal future (70 percent);

- Family support (64 percent);

- Participation in a religious community (64 percent);

- School engagement (64 percent); and

- Integrity (64 percent).

The assets that young people are least likely to experience include:

- Creative activities (19 percent);

- Community values youth (20 percent);

- Reading for pleasure (24 percent);

- Youth as resources (25 percent); and

- Caring school climate (25 percent).

The fact that most youth in all communities lack many of the assets represents a disturbing critique of American society. The lack is so widespread and common that it is fruitless to expect families or schools to repair the developmental web on their own.

FIGURE 1

Youth Who Report Experiencing Each Level of Assets

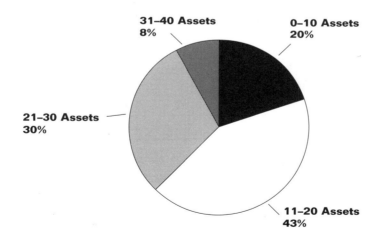

31–40 Assets
8%

0–10 Assets
20%

21–30 Assets
30%

11–20 Assets
43%

(Note: Numbers do not add to 100% due to rounding.)

Deficits and Risks in Young People's Lives

The gap between our ideal of all young people having more than 30 of the 40 assets and the reality described by these survey results suggests that many young people do not have the strengths and resources they need to thrive. Equally disturbing are the realities surrounding many of the risks young people face. This study focuses on two types of challenges:

- **Developmental deficits** (such as being home alone, experiencing physical abuse, and being a victim of violence), which may be liabilities in themselves but also increase the odds that young people will engage in high-risk behaviors.

- **High-risk behavior patterns** (such as repeatedly using alcohol and other drugs, being sexually active, engaging in multiple acts of violence, and gambling), which potentially limit psychological, physical, or economic health and well-being during adolescence and adulthood.

Figure 2 shows the percentages of youth who report each of the five deficits. Only 15 percent of young people surveyed experience none of the deficits. One-third of youth (32%) experience three or more. Reports of three deficits (victim of violence, TV overexposure, and physical abuse) increase through the middle school years, then decline through high school. The other two (drinking parties and alone at home) are more common for 12th graders than 6th graders.

When we look at young people's involvement in high-risk behavior patterns, we find that none of the high-risk behavior patterns is reported by more than one-third of young people (Figure 3). However, two of every three young people report engaging in at least 1 of the 10 high-risk behavior patterns. And by 12th grade, 50 percent of youth report engaging in 3 or more of the 10 patterns.

FIGURE 2

Youth Who Report Experiencing Developmental Deficits, in Descending Order

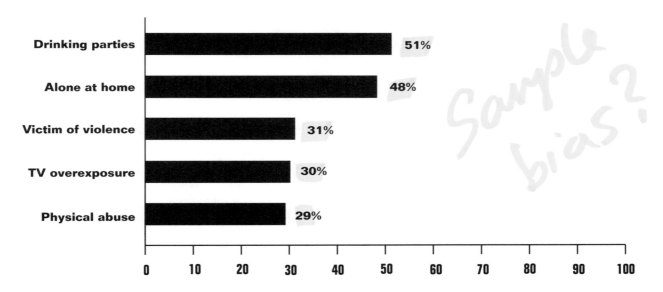

FIGURE 3

Youth Reporting Involvement in High-Risk Behavior Patterns, in Descending Order

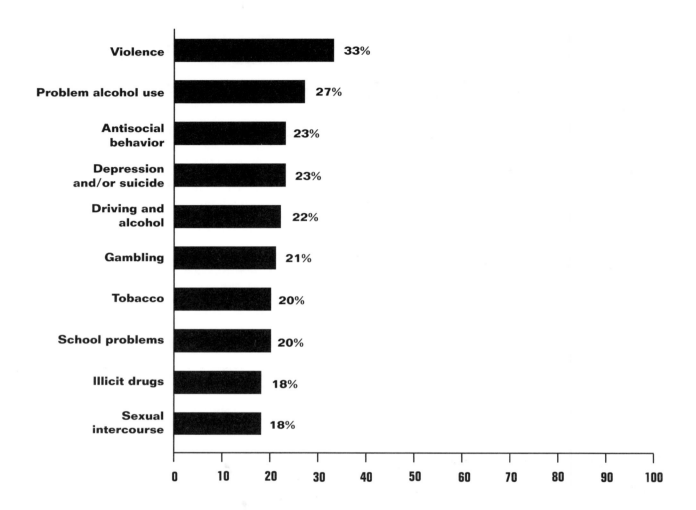

Evidence of Thriving

This study looks beyond whether young people avoid deficits and risks, and examines also the evidence that young people are developing in optimal ways. Thriving indicators suggest that young people are doing more than just surviving; they are acting in ways that make possible the development of their full potential.

The average young person reports having slightly more than half of the eight thriving indicators measured in this study. As Figure 4 shows, some indicators are quite common, such as overcomes adversity, while others (succeeds in school and resists danger) are experienced by only a minority of youth.

FIGURE 4

Youth Who Report Experiencing Thriving Indicators, in Descending Order

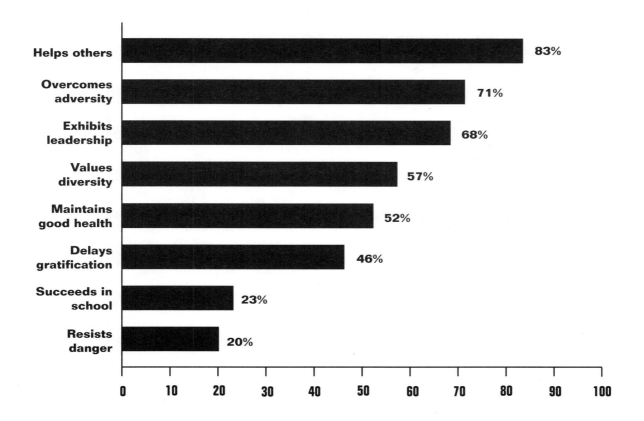

The Power of Developmental Assets

The developmental assets offer a positive, hopeful response to the challenges and risks young people face. They appear to play three critical roles in young people's lives.

1. They serve as **protective factors,** helping to "inoculate" youth against many forms of high-risk behavior.

2. They serve as **enhancement factors,** increasing the probability that youth will engage in thriving behaviors.

3. They help youth weather adversity, serving as **resiliency factors** that assist youth in minimizing the negative impact of deficits that can interfere with healthy development.

The power of assets is evident when we examine the responses of young people with only 0 to 10 assets (low-asset youth) in comparison to those young people who experience 31 to 40 of the assets (high-asset youth). We consistently see that low-asset youth are much more likely to engage in high-risk behaviors than high-asset youth. (See, for example, Figure 5a.) In addition, low-asset youth are much less likely to engage in any of the thriving behaviors than high-asset youth. (See, for example, Figure 5b.)

The power of assets to shape behavior is evident in all groups of youth, regardless of age, gender, race/ethnicity, family composition, family income level, and community size. All youth would benefit from experiencing more assets.

FIGURE 5

Examples of the Consequences of Developmental Assets

A. Problem Alcohol Use, by Level of Assets

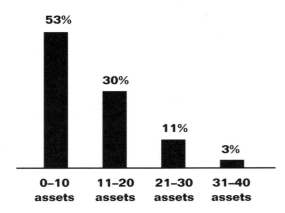

Percentage of youth reporting they have used alcohol three or more times in the past 30 days or have gotten drunk once or more in the past two weeks.

B. Succeeding in School, by Level of Assets

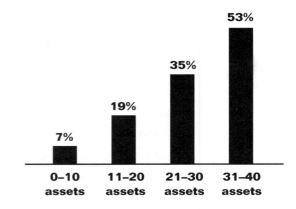

Percentage of youth reporting they get mostly A's on their report card.

Postscript

A number of trends in American culture contribute to the troubling patterns outlined in this report. They include the isolation of families, adult disengagement from community life and the lives of children and youth, the overprofessionalization of caring for young people, and a lack of consistency across the socializing systems in young people's lives.

Yet while these patterns are quite entrenched in this society, emerging signs of hope suggest that we are ready for the challenge.

1. The past 30 years have seen a dramatic increase in the knowledge of factors contributing to healthy development.

2. Many of the cultures that are part of this society offer wisdom, stories, and strengths that can be retold, renewed, and applied to the challenges our young people face.

3. Children's issues are high on the public and private agenda of the American people.

4. Many initiatives—large and small—are exploring innovative ways to call Americans to new levels of responsibility for children and adolescents.

Each of these signs can point us toward new ways to address the cultural obstacles to healthy development. But they are only beginning points. The challenge is to build and maintain a deep, lasting momentum and energy that gradually shifts the currents and transforms the culture into one that values, supports, and guides all young people to reach their full potential.

List of Figures and Tables

FIGURES

TABLES

Identifying and Measuring Developmental Assets

One of the most pressing social issues we face in the United States is how to provide all children and adolescents with a solid foundation for life. The evidence that the foundation is fragile appears year after year in newspaper articles and scientific studies that call attention to the challenges and problems facing too many youth: persistently high rates of alcohol and other drug use, teenage pregnancy, violence, school failure, and many others. Simultaneously, newer concerns are being voiced about whether we are building the kinds of skills and competencies needed to ensure a competent work force and an engaged citizenry. Put simply, we are failing to offer our youngest generations the solid footing they need to grow safely and successfully into adulthood.

People everywhere are looking for solutions. The most common response is to identify problems (e.g., chemical use, delinquency, school dropout, teen pregnancy, violence) and then seek to reduce them through prevention programs, early intervention, and social services. When problems persist, communities turn to increasingly expensive treatment and/or incarceration, further straining community resources and patience.

It is important to try to control and reduce problems. However, the problem-centered approach rarely works by itself. Despite the best intentions and valiant efforts of concerned and competent people and organizations (and some definite progress in reducing some problems among particular groups of youth), the problems remain too common for too many young people.

A complementary approach is needed—one that focuses on positive factors that contribute to healthy development. These factors can build up the strengths needed to help young people overcome the challenges and problems that can threaten their well-being. These same strengths can help make young people more likely to thrive.

A Fragile Foundation: The State of Developmental Assets among American Youth underscores the importance of focusing on strengths. It shows that many of the core processes of healthy development are absent for too many young people. The result is that young people build their futures on a fragile foundation, leading to many of the behavioral choices that trouble communities.

Naming the Positive:
The Framework of Developmental Assets

In an effort to identify the elements of a strength-based approach to healthy development, Search Institute developed the framework of developmental assets (Table 1.1). This framework identifies 40 factors of young people's growth and development. Together, the assets offer a set of benchmarks for positive child and adolescent development. The assets clearly show important roles that families, schools, congregations, neighborhoods, youth organizations, and others in communities play in shaping young people's lives.

When present, these 40 assets help protect youth against high-risk behavior and help increase positive developmental outcomes. By focusing on building these assets among all children and adolescents, communities have the potential not only to lessen high-risk behavior but also to nurture a generation of competent, caring, and successful young people.

TABLE 1.1

40 Developmental Assets

EXTERNAL ASSETS		INTERNAL ASSETS	
CATEGORY	**ASSET NAME AND DEFINITION**	**CATEGORY**	**ASSET NAME AND DEFINITION**

EXTERNAL ASSETS

Support

1. **Family support**—Family life provides high levels of love and support.
2. **Positive family communication**—Young person and her or his parent(s) communicate positively, and young person is willing to seek advice and counsel from parent(s).
3. **Other adult relationships**—Young person receives support from three or more nonparent adults.
4. **Caring neighborhood**—Young person experiences caring neighbors.
5. **Caring school climate**—School provides a caring, encouraging environment.
6. **Parent involvement in schooling**—Parent(s) are actively involved in helping young person succeed in school.

Empowerment

7. **Community values youth**—Young person perceives that adults in the community value youth.
8. **Youth as resources**—Young people are given useful roles in the community.
9. **Service to others**—Young person serves in the community one hour or more per week.
10. **Safety**—Young person feels safe at home, at school, and in the neighborhood.

Boundaries and Expectations

11. **Family boundaries**—Family has clear rules and consequences and monitors the young person's whereabouts.
12. **School boundaries**—School provides clear rules and consequences.
13. **Neighborhood boundaries**—Neighbors take responsibility for monitoring young people's behavior.
14. **Adult role models**—Parent(s) and other adults model positive, responsible behavior.
15. **Positive peer influence**—Young person's best friends model responsible behavior.
16. **High expectations**—Both parent(s) and teachers encourage the young person to do well.

Constructive Use of Time

17. **Creative activities**—Young person spends three or more hours per week in lessons or practice in music, theater, or other arts.
18. **Youth programs**—Young person spends three or more hours per week in sports, clubs, or organizations at school and/or in the community.
19. **Religious community**—Young person spends one or more hours per week in activities in a religious institution.
20. **Time at home**—Young person is out with friends "with nothing special to do" two or fewer nights per week.

INTERNAL ASSETS

Commitment to Learning

21. **Achievement motivation**—Young person is motivated to do well in school.
22. **School engagement**—Young person is actively engaged in learning.
23. **Homework**—Young person reports doing at least one hour of homework every school day.
24. **Bonding to school**—Young person cares about her or his school.
25. **Reading for pleasure**—Young person reads for pleasure three or more hours per week.

Positive Values

26. **Caring**—Young person places high value on helping other people.
27. **Equality and social justice**—Young person places high value on promoting equality and reducing hunger and poverty.
28. **Integrity**—Young person acts on convictions and stands up for her or his beliefs.
29. **Honesty**—Young person "tells the truth even when it is not easy."
30. **Responsibility**—Young person accepts and takes personal responsibility.
31. **Restraint**—Young person believes it is important not to be sexually active or to use alcohol or other drugs.

Social Competencies

32. **Planning and decision making**—Young person knows how to plan ahead and make choices.
33. **Interpersonal competence**—Young person has empathy, sensitivity, and friendship skills.
34. **Cultural competence**—Young person has knowledge of and comfort with people of different cultural/racial/ethnic backgrounds.
35. **Resistance skills**—Young person can resist negative peer pressure and dangerous situations.
36. **Peaceful conflict resolution**—Young person seeks to resolve conflict nonviolently.

Positive Identity

37. **Personal power**—Young person feels he or she has control over "things that happen to me."
38. **Self-esteem**—Young person reports having a high self-esteem.
39. **Sense of purpose**—Young person reports that "my life has a purpose."
40. **Positive view of personal future**—Young person is optimistic about her or his personal future.

External Assets

The first 20 developmental assets focus on positive experiences that young people receive from the people and institutions in their lives. Four categories of external assets are included in the framework:

- **Support**—Young people need to experience support, care, and love from their families and many others. They need organizations and institutions that provide positive, supportive environments.

- **Empowerment**—Young people need to be valued by their community and have opportunities to contribute to others. For this to occur, they must be safe and feel secure.

- **Boundaries and expectations**—Young people need to know what is expected of them and whether activities and behaviors are "in bounds" or "out of bounds."

- **Constructive use of time**—Young people need constructive, enriching opportunities for growth through creative activities, youth programs, congregational involvement, and quality time at home.

In a healthy community, young people experience these external assets consistently, many times, and in many places. Families, volunteers, neighborhoods, schools, community organizations, the businesses that employ parents and adolescents, sports and recreation programs, and religious institutions all play roles in providing these positive experiences. In addition, young people experience the external assets through informal, daily interactions with caring and principled peers and adults.

Internal Assets

A community's responsibility for its young people does not end with the provision of external assets. A similar commitment is required for nurturing the internal qualities that guide choices and create a sense of centeredness, purpose, and focus. Indeed, shaping internal dispositions that encourage wise, responsible, and compassionate judgments is particularly important in a society that prizes individualism. Four categories of internal assets are included in the framework:

- **Commitment to learning**—Young people need to develop a lifelong commitment to education and learning.

- **Positive values**—Youth need to develop strong values that guide their choices.

- **Social competencies**—Young people need skills and competencies that equip them to make positive choices, build relationships, and succeed in life.

- **Positive identity**—Young people need a strong sense of their own power, purpose, worth, and promise.

These assets do not develop automatically. Like external assets, internal assets emerge best when people consistently pay attention to these crucial building blocks. Ideally, the residents of a town or city share a commitment to encouraging all young people to learn, modeling values and self-improvement efforts, and teaching competencies needed for adult success. Such commitment is evidenced when many sectors of community life—families, informal networks, schools, youth organizations, media, religious institutions, places of employment, neighborhoods—work hand in hand to continually encourage and promote these assets.

Background on the Developmental Assets

Researchers have learned a great deal in the past several decades about elements in human experience that have long-term, positive consequences for young people. Factors such as family dynamics, support from community adults, school effectiveness, peer influence, values clarification, and social skills have all been identified as contributing to healthy development. However, these different areas of study are typically disconnected from each other.

The framework of developmental assets steps back to look at the whole—to pull many pieces together into a comprehensive vision of what young people need to thrive. With roots in the scientific research on adolescent development, the assets grow out of two types of applied research:

- **Prevention,** which focuses on protective factors that inhibit high-risk behaviors such as substance abuse, violence, too-early sexual intercourse, and dropping out of school; and

- **Resiliency,** which identifies factors that increase young people's ability to rebound in the face of adversity, from poverty to drug-abusing parents to dangerous neighborhoods.

The developmental asset framework and terminology were first introduced in 1990 in a Search Institute report titled *The Troubled Journey: A Portrait of 6th-12th Grade Youth.* At that time, the survey identified and measured 30 developmental assets. We continued to review the research, as well as conduct our own studies, cumulatively surveying more than 350,000 6th-12th graders in more than 600 communities between 1990 and 1995 to learn about the developmental assets they experienced, the risks they took, the deficits they had to overcome, and the ways they thrived.

We also conducted numerous informal discussions and focus groups with professionals and practitioners in youth-related fields, in particular to better understand the developmental realities of youth of color and youth in distressed communities. Those focus groups led us to elaborate more on safety and cultural competence as assets in adolescence. As a result of all these ongoing research activities, in 1996 we revised the developmental asset framework into its current form, a model of 40 developmental assets. (For more scientific information on the development, measurement, and content of the framework of developmental assets, see the scientific resources listed at the end of this chapter.)

Although originally developed with a focus on adolescents, the basic framework of developmental assets is relevant for all young people from birth through age 18. A 1997 Search Institute report, *Starting Out Right: Developmental Assets for Children,* extended the framework to younger children, showing developmentally specific ways each asset contributes to healthy development in the first decade of life.[1]

---

[1] Nancy Leffert, Peter L. Benson, and Jolene L. Roehlkepartain, *Starting Out Right: Developmental Assets for Children* (Minneapolis: Search Institute, 1997).

Principles Undergirding the Asset Framework

The asset framework is not the final or complete authority on factors that contribute to young people's healthy development. New studies regularly compel researchers to revise their theories and models, and this framework is no exception to that rule. But whether the original 30-asset framework, the current 40-asset approach, or a future model, several filters or principles have guided and will continue to guide the identification of assets to include.

Research support

Each of the developmental assets grows out of a body of scientific literature that shows its positive impact in young people's lives. Search Institute recently completed an extensive review and synthesis of more than 800 relevant research articles and reports. We concluded that, although the developmental assets framework, like any approach, has areas of both strength and weakness, it is remarkably representative of and consistent with the scientific literature on adolescent development. The experiences and qualities captured in the framework have generally been well established by other researchers, both in terms of preventing risky behavior and promoting positive behavior.[2]

All youth

A critical principle that guides the asset framework is that assets are about what all youth need to succeed. Not just "at-risk" youth. Not just youth living in poverty. Whether male or female, rich or poor, gay or straight, White, African American, Latina/Latino, Asian American, American Indian, or multiracial, all youth need these building blocks in order to construct a strong foundation for their lives. Different populations of young people may experience the assets differently and have different patterns of assets. And particular assets may have different meanings depending on the circumstances in which young people live. Nonetheless, the basic experiences are relevant to all youth.

By focusing on all youth, the model does not take into account some positive experiences that are particularly relevant within specific cultures and traditions. Excluding these experiences is not intended to devalue them; rather, they are simply excluded by the process of identifying a common core of positive experiences, qualities, and relationships that unifies people across differences.

---

[2] Peter C. Scales and Nancy Leffert, *Developmental Assets: A Synthesis of the Scientific Research on Adolescent Development* (Minneapolis: Search Institute, 1999).

Relationships and environments

The framework focuses on *basic, positive socialization processes,* what we have called the developmental infrastructure, as contrasted with the physical, human services, or economic infrastructure of communities. We do not view the latter as unimportant. Instead, we focus on the relationships, social experiences, social environments, interactions, and norms over which the community has a greater measure of control. Human development complements economic development. It doesn't replace it.

Power to mobilize

The focus on the socialization processes in young people's lives leads to increased attention to how every person and every institution can contribute to young people's healthy development. Although professionals and the public sector have important roles to play, much of the responsibility and capacity for the healthy development of youth is in the hands of all the individual people of our communities.

The asset framework attempts to more broadly define what is possible and to motivate people to take steps toward making the possible real. It is easier to visualize doing something positive than preventing something negative. So, by describing the positive things youth need, the framework gives typical residents more tangible and concrete ideas about what they personally can do.

Measuring the Assets

To this point, we have described how the asset framework has been conceptualized, based on available research as well as the experiences of practitioners. As important as this theoretical work is, we begin to see the real power and meaning in this conceptualization when we measure the presence—or absence—of these assets in young people's lives.

What the survey measures

Since 1989, Search Institute has conducted numerous studies of 6th- to 12th-grade students in public and private schools across the United States using a survey titled *Profiles of Student Life: Attitudes and Behaviors.* The survey was revised in 1996 to reflect the expansion of the asset framework from 30 to 40 assets. The current survey has 156 items that measure the extent to which an individual student responds that he or she experiences:

- Each of the **40 developmental assets;**

- **Developmental deficits** (e.g., physical abuse, spending too much time alone, watching too much television);

- **Risky behaviors and high-risk behavior patterns,** including alcohol, tobacco, and other drug use, school failure, and attempted suicide; and

- **Thriving indicators,** including succeeding in school and maintaining good health.

Appendixes A-D contain tables that show each of the developmental assets, developmental deficits, high-risk behavior patterns, and thriving behaviors that are measured in the survey, their definitions, and an item mapping of the survey questions.

By assessing all these elements simultaneously, we gain a broad description of young people's development and life experiences. This broad approach limits the amount of detail and depth we can measure; to gain a deeper understanding of each element, we would need to ask many questions about each element. However, the advantage of this broad approach is that it shows the connections and relationships among the different areas of young people's experiences and lives.[3]

In some ways, it is like the difference between looking at a world map and a country map. The world map helps you see all the countries and how they relate to each other geographically; the country map helps you get a much deeper understanding of that specific country. Thus, many other researchers have done extensive "mapping" of individual areas of young people's lives (the country maps). The asset framework is like a world map that helps put all the pieces in perspective with each other and joins them in a meaningful global view.

---

[3] Details on the measurement of the assets, risks, deficits, and thriving indicators are found in Appendixes A, B, C, and D. See also Nancy Leffert, Peter L. Benson, Peter C. Scales, Anu R. Sharma, Dyanne R. Drake, and Dale A. Blyth, "Developmental Assets: Measurement and Prediction of Risk Behaviors among Adolescents," *Applied Developmental Science, 2* (1998), 209-230.

How the data were gathered

Communities represented in this study conducted through schools or community initiatives the *Search Institute Profiles of Student Life: Attitudes and Behaviors* survey. The process is as follows[4]:

1. Schools contact Search Institute and ask to conduct the survey, often as part of a community-wide asset-building initiative.

2. Search Institute sends the survey instruments to schools, along with instructions for how to administer them.

3. Teachers distribute and collect the surveys in their classrooms, using standardized procedures.

4. Surveys are returned to Search Institute.

5. Search Institute analyzes the data and prepares a report that is sent back to the school district for use in its own planning.

Ensuring the quality of the data

People often ask how we know young people are telling the truth when they complete this survey. While there is no way to guarantee honesty on a self-report survey, several things are done to increase our confidence in the quality of the data:

- The surveys are anonymous and confidential, with no student identification number or other identifying information on them. Students in each classroom place their own completed surveys in a single envelope that is then sealed and mailed to Search Institute, so no one within a school ever sees an individual student's survey.

- Several strategies are used to discard surveys that clearly show young people are responding inconsistently or dishonestly, including discarding surveys with 40 or more unanswered questions.

Criteria for inclusion in aggregate sample

Not every community that used the survey is included in this aggregate sample. The schools included in the sample that undergirds this report met the following criteria:

- The surveys were conducted by public or alternative schools during the 1996–97 school year.

- There was low student absenteeism on the day the survey was administered.

- At least one grade from grades 6 to 9 *and* one from grades 10 to 12 were surveyed. (Not all communities administered the survey to all students in grades 6 to 7. But a comparison of data from schools that surveyed all grades with those that surveyed just one grade in each range showed few differences.)

---

[4] For more information on the costs and procedures of this survey service, contact Search Institute, 800-888-7828.

About the Sample

The data presented in this report are based on a sample of 99,462 6th- to 12th-grade students in public and/or alternative schools who completed the *Search Institute Profiles of Student Life: Attitudes and Behaviors* (A&B) survey during the 1996-97 school year. The sample includes surveys from 213 U.S. communities in 25 states.

Table 1.2 presents the demographic composition of this sample. Because this sample is drawn from individual communities that chose to survey their own students, it is not nationally representative. For example, this aggregate sample overrepresents White youth from smaller cities and towns whose parents have a higher-than-average level of formal education. Furthermore, the sample is largely from Midwestern communities. This sample nevertheless is large and diverse, and provides a sense of how youth in a significant number of communities describe their lives. Several factors give us confidence that the findings are meaningful and generalizable.

First, this sample is just a part of the more than 500,000 6th- to 12th-grade youth in more than 600 communities whom we have surveyed since 1989. The findings in this report are remarkably similar to the results from the larger aggregation of youth, despite the fact that some youth completed survey instruments that were based on the original 30-asset framework, and some on the current 40-asset framework.

Second, the responses from the aggregate sample on specific questions are very similar to national figures on various risky behaviors. For example, Table 1.3 compares several risky behaviors among 9th- to 12th-grade youth from our sample with the 9th- to 12th-grade youth surveyed in the 1997 *Youth Risk Behavior Surveillance* (YRBS) survey conducted by the U.S. Centers for Disease Control and Prevention. The A&B sample shows about the same level of alcohol and cigarette use as the YRBS sample, and only a little less violent behavior. Our sample has a higher proportion of youth who report ever having attempted suicide, but a lower proportion of youth who report ever having had sexual intercourse.

Despite those similarities to some national figures, we believe, on the basis of the nonrepresentative nature of the sample, that the data in this book probably *overstate* how many assets and thriving indicators young people in the United States have, and probably *understate* youth deficits and high-risk behavior patterns. If anything, the national situation is probably worse.

TABLE 1.2

Composition of the 1996-97 Aggregate Sample

	Sample Size*	% of Total
Total	99,462	100
Grade		
6	9,861	10
7	15,093	15
8	15,298	15
9	18,411	19
10	15,946	16
11	13,963	14
12	10,777	11
Gender		
Female	49,138	50
Male	49,620	50
Race/Ethnicity		
African American	1,594	2
Asian American	1,988	2
Latina/Latino	4,152	4
Multiracial	4,505	5
Native American	1,563	2
White	84,816	86
Type of Community		
Farm	9,018	9
Country (nonfarm)	16,657	17
American Indian reservation	796	1
Small town (under 2,500 in population)	14,601	15
Town of 2,500 to 9,999	18,257	19
Small city (10,000 to 49,999)	20,550	22
Medium city (50,000 to 250,000)	12,201	13
Large city (over 250,000)	3,450	4

	Sample Size*	% of Total
Region		
South	4,103	4
West	8,508	9
Midwest	81,275	82
East	5,404	5
Mother's Education		
Grade school	1,530	2
Some high school	5,183	5
High school graduate	27,017	28
Some college	16,935	18
College graduate	27,500	29
Graduate/professional school	11,219	12
Don't know/does not apply	6,172	7
Father's Education		
Grade school	1,852	2
Some high school	6,266	7
High school graduate	25,740	27
Some college	14,619	15
College graduate	26,171	27
Graduate/professional school	12,243	13
Don't know/does not apply	8,579	9

*Totals may not sum to 99,462 due to missing data.

TABLE 1.3

Comparison of Data from Self-Reports of Involvement in Risky Behaviors from the YRBS Survey and the A&B Survey (9th- to 12th-Grade Youth)*

	YRBS	A&B
Drinking alcohol in the past 30 days	51%	49%
Smoking cigarettes in the past 30 days	36%	39%
Ever having sexual intercourse	48%	39%
Ever attempting suicide	8%	16%
Hitting someone in a fight in the past 12 months	37%	32%
Carrying a weapon in the past 12 months	18%	11%

*YRBS = 1997 *Youth Risk Behavior Surveillance Survey* conducted by the U.S. Centers for Disease Control and Prevention; A&B = Search Institute's aggregate sample of students who completed the *Search Institute Profiles of Student Life: Attitudes and Behaviors* survey during the 1996-97 school year.

What This Research Contributes

The framework of developmental assets has two major uses. First, it is designed, in part, to motivate and connect people, organizations, and communities around a shared understanding of—and response to—young people's needs, accenting the essential elements of positive human development. Because of this broad goal, the research in this report is presented in nontechnical terms using analyses that communicate easily.

The second major use of this framework is to encourage a comprehensive research approach that examines multiple elements of human development. As this report will repeatedly show, the true power of the positive is not in each isolated element but in adding all the elements together. Much more needs to be learned about these dynamics. We hope this report stimulates dialogue, debate, and additional research that will, in time, refine our understanding of the building blocks young people need to construct a solid foundation for life.

Scientific Resources on Developmental Assets

Benson, Peter L., Nancy Leffert, Peter C. Scales, and Dale A. Blyth. "Beyond the 'Village' Rhetoric: Creating Healthy Communities for Children and Adolescents." *Applied Developmental Science, 2* (1998), 138-159.

Blyth, Dale A., and Nancy Leffert. "Communities as Contexts for Adolescent Development: An Empirical Analysis." *Journal of Adolescent Research, 10* (1995), 64-87.

Leffert, Nancy, Peter L. Benson, Peter C. Scales, Anu R. Sharma, Dyanne R. Drake, and Dale A. Blyth. "Developmental Assets: Measurement and Prediction of Risk Behaviors among Adolescents." *Applied Developmental Science, 2* (1998), 209-230.

Scales, Peter C., Peter L. Benson, Nancy Leffert, and Dale A. Blyth (in press). "The Strength of Developmental Assets as Predictors of Positive Youth Development Outcomes." *Applied Developmental Science.*

Scales, Peter C., and Nancy Leffert. *Developmental Assets: A Synthesis of the Scientific Research on Adolescent Development* (Minneapolis: Search Institute, 1999).

2

Young People's Experiences of Developmental Assets

Chapter 1 introduced the vision and background of the developmental assets. In this chapter, we look at how young people experience—or do not experience—these assets. Thus, it identifies areas of strength as well as gaps in young people's experience that, as we'll see in later chapters, contribute to many of the vexing problems society faces regarding our young people.

This chapter begins by examining each of the eight categories of external and internal assets, showing how the young people we surveyed actually experience each of these 40 assets. In the process, it highlights similarities and differences among different populations of youth, including age and gender differences. Some racial/ethnic differences are also noted (and shown in detail in Appendix A), though we do so with more caution because, as noted in Chapter 1, this sample underrepresents people of color.

As interesting and helpful as it is to understand some of the details in differences among reports of individual assets from different populations of youth, the true power of the asset framework comes as the pieces are pulled together, by looking at the overall experiences of young people in light of the assets. So the second part of this chapter takes a broader view, showing overall patterns in young people's experience of the assets. This perspective sets the stage for understanding the cumulative power of developmental assets and the importance of a comprehensive, community-wide strategy for asset building.

We turn, then, to an exploration of the eight categories of assets.

Support

The first category of assets is support. Support refers to a range of ways in which young people experience love, affirmation, and acceptance. Ideally, young people experience an abundance of this kind of support not only in their families but also from many people across many settings, including neighborhoods and schools.

Other adult relationships (asset #3) and caring neighborhood (asset #4) hold up the importance of intergenerational relationships. Ideally, children and teenagers should have sustained relationships with many adults beyond their immediate family, including aunts and uncles, grandparents, teachers, neighbors, formal and informal mentors, coaches, youth workers, and employers. Such relationships are crucial for nurturing self-esteem, building social competencies, and transmitting important cultural values. Intergenerational, nonfamily relationships become even more important when parents are less often with their children because of work, separation, or divorce.

Key findings

- Support is fragile in every community studied. Indeed, five of the six support assets are experienced by less than half of the youth surveyed.

- With the exception of other adult relationships (asset #3), reports of all the support assets decline through the middle and high school years. Reports of other adult relationships increase slightly.

- Overall, females and males report very similar levels of all the support assets.

- Three support assets are experienced by only about one in five 12th graders: #5, caring school climate (23 percent), #2, positive family communication (19 percent), and #6, parent involvement in schooling (17 percent).

- While family support (asset #1) is among the most commonly experienced assets, it is striking that one-third of the young people surveyed do not experience this fundamental asset in their homes.

Why is support so uncommon for today's young people? Several factors could be at work. First, the extreme age segregation that dominates current American culture inhibits the dynamic transmission of human wisdom and knowledge from the elders of a society to its youngest members.

Another factor is the widespread misperception of adolescence and adolescents in our culture. Parents are given messages that adolescence is inevitably a "turbulent" time and that their children do not want parents around. In addition, as teenagers become more physically independent, they rely less on their parents, so it is easy for parents to become less involved in their children's lives, including their schools. Yet research clearly shows the importance of maintaining close relationships and staying involved, even while the child is becoming more independent and autonomous.

FIGURE 2.1

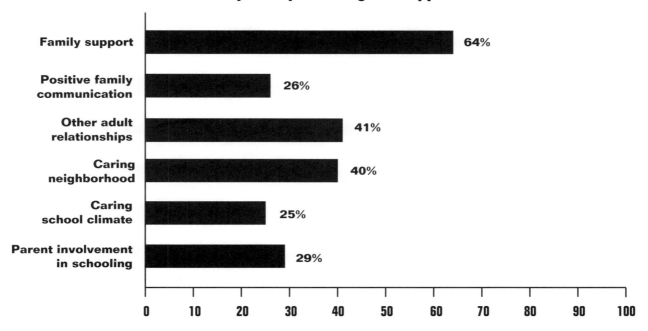

Youth Who Report Experiencing the Support Assets

TABLE 2.1

Youth Who Report Experiencing the Support Assets, by Grade and Gender (in %)

ASSET		ALL	GRADE						
			6	7	8	9	10	11	12
1. Family support	All	64	79	73	64	60	58	59	60
	Females	65	80	73	64	60	59	60	62
	Males	64	79	73	64	61	58	58	57
2. Positive family communication	All	26	40	33	27	25	22	20	19
	Females	28	44	35	29	26	24	21	20
	Males	24	37	30	25	23	20	19	17
3. Other adult relationships	All	41	41	41	39	39	40	42	46
	Females	43	45	44	42	41	41	43	47
	Males	39	36	37	36	38	38	41	45
4. Caring neighborhood	All	40	50	45	41	38	37	34	35
	Females	41	53	48	43	40	38	35	35
	Males	38	47	43	39	36	35	34	34
5. Caring school climate	All	25	38	30	24	21	20	20	23
	Females	27	43	34	27	23	22	22	25
	Males	22	34	26	21	19	18	19	21
6. Parent involvement in schooling	All	29	45	40	32	28	23	20	17
	Females	29	44	40	31	28	24	22	19
	Males	29	45	41	32	28	23	19	15

Empowerment

The empowerment assets relate to the key developmental need for youth to be valued and feel valuable. The empowerment assets highlight this need, focusing on community perceptions of youth (as reported by youth) and opportunities for youth to contribute to society in meaningful ways.

The perception of safety (asset #10) is an important underlying factor of youth empowerment. Students who feel safe are more likely to feel valued and able to make a difference than students who feel afraid at home, at school, or in the neighborhood. It is an ideal that our children deserve but one that is too rarely achieved.

Key findings

- The percentage of youth who experience two of the four empowerment assets is quite low. Only 20 percent of youth surveyed perceive their community as a place that values youth (asset #7, one of the assets least reported by youth), and only 25 percent report being given useful roles to play within community life (asset #8)

- Half of all youth say they are involved in service to others, with females being more likely than males to report this involvement (asset #9).

- Whereas we might hope (and assume) that young people who are older are more likely to be valued as contributors to their communities, the opposite is true, from young people's point of view. Their reports of the first three empowerment assets all decline across the years. Only reports of the safety asset increase across the years.

- Just over half of all the youth surveyed report experiencing safety in their homes, schools, and neighborhoods. Females are quite a bit less likely to report feeling safe.

Many adults are surprised when they see that only one in five young people say their community values youth. Yet young people in all types of communities tell stories of suspicious looks, mistrust, looking away, and being ill-treated. These perceptions are reinforced by the findings of a 1997 Public Agenda report, *Kids These Days: What Americans Really Think about the Next Generation:* "When asked what first comes to their minds when they think about today's teenagers, two-thirds of Americans (67 percent) immediately reach for negative adjectives such as 'rude,' 'irresponsible,' and 'wild'. . . . Only a handful (12 percent) describe teenagers positively, using terms such as 'smart' or 'helpful'."[1] Our survey findings show that young people are clearly aware of and familiar with these prevalent attitudes.

---

[1] Steve Farkas and Jean Johnson, *Kids These Days: What Americans Really Think about the Next Generation* (New York: Public Agenda, 1997), 8.

FIGURE 2.2

Youth Who Report Experiencing the Empowerment Assets

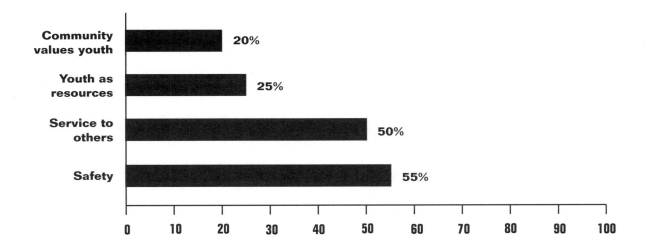

TABLE 2.2

Youth Who Report Experiencing the Empowerment Assets, by Grade and Gender (in %)

ASSET		ALL	GRADE						
			6	7	8	9	10	11	12
7. Community values youth	All	20	33	26	21	17	15	15	16
	Females	21	37	29	22	18	16	15	17
	Males	19	29	24	10	16	14	14	16
8. Youth as resources	All	25	36	32	25	23	20	19	19
	Females	25	37	33	26	22	21	19	20
	Males	24	34	31	25	23	20	19	19
9. Service to others	All	50	61	56	51	48	46	44	45
	Females	55	67	62	56	53	51	49	51
	Males	45	56	51	46	44	40	38	39
10. Safety	All	55	45	46	51	52	57	65	68
	Females	47	40	41	45	44	47	54	57
	Males	63	50	52	58	60	67	76	80

Boundaries and Expectations

Boundaries-and-expectations assets highlight young people's need for clear and enforced standards and norms to complement support and empowerment. They need to know what kinds of behaviors are "in bounds" and what kinds are "out of bounds." Ideally, young people experience appropriate boundaries in their families, schools, and neighborhoods (as well as other settings), receiving a set of consistent messages about acceptable behavior across socializing systems.

High expectations are likewise important for young people. High expectations can challenge young people to excel and can enhance their sense of being capable. Adult role models provide another important source for modeling what communities deem important. Finally, although peer pressure is most often viewed negatively, peers can also play a positive role in helping shape behavior in healthy ways.

Key findings

- While clear and consistent boundary messages are crucial, only a minority of youth report experiencing such clear boundary messages in their families, their schools, and their neighborhoods. Only one boundaries-and-expectations asset (#15, positive peer influence) is reported by most youth.

- Young people are twice as likely to report peers being a positive influence (60 percent) as they are to report having positive adult role models (27 percent, asset #14).

- Reports of all the boundaries-and-expectations assets decline between 6th and 12th grades. Some loosening or renegotiation of boundaries is developmentally appropriate. However, some of these assets—such as positive peer influence, adult role models, and high expectations—should not decline.

- Females report experiencing five of these six assets more than males do, with the greatest differences being on neighborhood boundaries (an 11-percentage-point difference, asset #13) and positive peer influence (a 10-percentage-point difference).

Several dynamics may be shaping young people's experiences of these assets. First, as noted in the discussion of support, parents and others tend to decrease the level of monitoring of young people's behavior as they approach and enter late adolescence and early adulthood. This disengagement not only affects experiences of support, but also makes it more difficult to set, monitor, and enforce developmentally appropriate boundaries. While some separation is healthy—and inevitable—that need should not be mistaken for a reason to leave young people without guidance or boundaries.

Perhaps just as important is that this society does not have a shared understanding of what boundaries and expectations are appropriate for young people at various ages and which settings or socializing institutions should do the job. Too often, families alone are expected to be the place that establishes and enforces boundaries. Schools, neighborhoods, and other settings may be reluctant to establish and enforce boundaries that might be perceived as interfering with parental rights and responsibilities. Such tentativeness can only be overcome with open conversation about shared norms, values, and expectations within the community.

FIGURE 2.3

Youth Who Report Experiencing the Boundaries-and-Expectations Assets

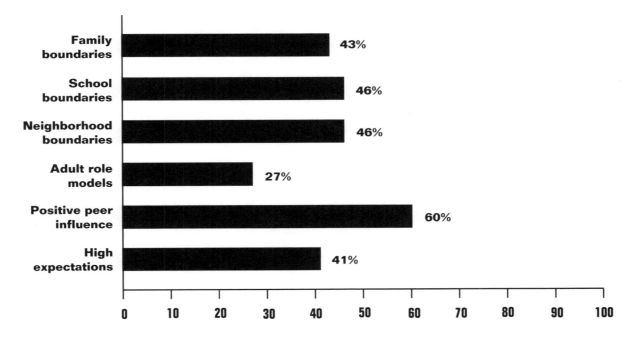

TABLE 2.3

Youth Who Report Experiencing the Boundaries-and-Expectations Assets, by Grade and Gender (in %)

ASSET		ALL	GRADE						
			6	7	8	9	10	11	12
11. Family boundaries	All	43	49	47	43	43	43	41	34
	Females	46	50	49	46	46	46	44	38
	Males	40	47	44	40	40	40	37	30
12. School boundaries	All	46	70	58	50	42	37	36	34
	Females	49	72	61	53	44	40	39	39
	Males	43	68	56	47	40	34	33	30
13. Neighborhood boundaries	All	46	59	54	49	44	41	39	35
	Females	56	61	55	49	44	41	39	36
	Males	45	58	54	48	45	41	39	35
14. Adult role models	All	27	35	32	26	25	24	25	26
	Females	31	40	36	30	27	27	29	31
	Males	23	30	27	22	22	21	20	22
15. Positive peer influence	All	60	82	75	62	56	51	49	49
	Females	65	87	79	66	59	56	55	56
	Males	55	77	71	58	52	46	43	42
16. High expectations	All	41	59	51	43	37	35	33	33
	Females	41	58	51	43	37	35	34	35
	Males	41	60	51	43	37	35	33	32

Constructive Use of Time

One of the prime characteristics of a healthy community for youth is a rich array of structured opportunities for children and adolescents. Whether through schools, community organizations, or religious institutions, these structured activities contribute to the development of many of the assets. They not only help build young people's peer relationships and skills, but they also connect youth to principled, caring adults.

In addition, structured time use can serve as a constructive alternative to the idle time now common for youth. Such idle time, while not always unproductive or dangerous, increases the probability of negative peer influence and overexposure to the mass media.

The need for these activities might be balanced with the need to spend time at home (asset #20), relaxing, reconnecting, reflecting, and participating in family life.

Key findings

- Three of the four constructive-use-of-time assets are experienced by half or more of the youth surveyed.

- However, creative activities (asset #17) is the least reported of all the 40 assets. And while 24 percent of females are involved in creative activities, only 14 percent of males are.

- With the exception of reports of involvement in youth programs (asset #18), which remain relatively stable across the grades, reports of all the other constructive-use-of-time assets decline between 6th and 12th grades.

- While the percentage of young people reporting involvement in religious community (asset #19) is higher than for other types of activities, note that this asset is scored as present based on *one* hour per week, while the others are scored as present based on *three* hours per week. Only 19 percent of youth report spending *three* or more hours per week in religious activities.

The overall percentages in this asset category may mask the existence of two distinct realities for youth. Some young people have many opportunities to participate in programs and activities. For them, the main message of these assets may be asset #20—the importance of being home and having times of solitude as an antidote to the stress and strain of a too-full schedule.

Most young people, however, face the opposite reality: little access to positive, safe, and enriching places to spend time outside of school. In these cases, communities—and society—must find ways to invest in opportunities that capture young people's interests and help them grow. In addition, efforts must be made to ensure that these opportunities are accessible and publicized so that the young people who would benefit from them can actually participate.

FIGURE 2.4

Youth Who Report Experiencing the Constructive-Use of-Time Assets

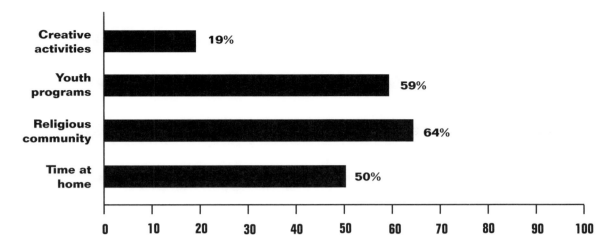

TABLE 2.4

Youth Who Report Experiencing the Constructive-Use-of-Time Assets, by Grade and Gender (in %)

ASSET		ALL	GRADE						
			6	7	8	9	10	11	12
17. Creative activities	All	19	23	21	20	18	17	17	15
	Females	24	31	27	26	23	22	20	18
	Males	14	16	15	14	13	13	14	13
18. Youth programs	All	59	57	60	60	60	58	57	57
	Females	58	57	60	59	59	59	57	57
	Males	59	57	60	61	61	57	58	58
19. Religious community	All	64	72	71	68	65	62	57	54
	Females	68	76	74	72	69	67	60	58
	Males	61	69	68	65	61	57	54	50
20. Time at home	All	50	57	56	51	51	47	43	42
	Females	51	59	58	51	52	48	44	45
	Males	48	55	55	50	50	46	41	39

Commitment to Learning

Commitment to learning is essential to young people in today's changing world. Developing intellectual curiosity and the skills to gain new knowledge and learn from experience is an important task for members of a workforce that must adapt to rapid change.

A commitment to learning can be nurtured in all young people, not just in those who excel academically. All young people need to discover the joy of learning about particular interests in ways that fit their learning styles and abilities. Only then will they develop the kind of commitment to learning that will help them continue to discover, grow, and learn throughout their lives.

The commitment-to-learning assets measure several dimensions of a young person's engagement with learning in school. In addition, they touch on informal, self-motivated learning and discovery through reading for pleasure (asset #25).

Key findings

- Three of the five commitment-to-learning assets are experienced by at least half of the youth surveyed. However, reading for pleasure (asset #24) is among the least reported of the 40 assets.

- Females are much more likely than males (at least a 10-percentage-point difference) to report all of the commitment-to-learning assets. The only commitment-to-learning asset that a majority of females do not report having is reading for pleasure (asset #25).

- Reports of achievement motivation (asset #21), bonding to school (asset #24), and reading for pleasure (asset #25) decline as young people advance through middle and high school.

- Reports of school engagement (asset #22) dip in the middle of the grade range and rise again, with the low point coming in 8th grade. Reports of homework (asset #23) climb through 11th grade, and then fall for 12th graders.

When we look at connections among all the assets, we see some relationships between the commitment-to-learning assets and positive school climate (asset #5 in support).[2] Students who see their school as a caring place are more likely to care about their school, to be interested in their schoolwork, and to try hard. This finding should remind us that if we want students to learn, we need to pay attention to more than "just the facts." Students are more likely to "get the facts"—to learn—when they can do so in an environment where they feel cared for and supported. These data reinforce other studies showing that all in the community—not only schools—need to do a better job of keeping students interested in learning.

---

[2] A caring school climate had a correlation of .40 with school engagement and .35 with bonding to school, among the strongest relationships of assets with each other. (For additional information, see Peter C. Scales and Nancy Leffert, *Developmental Assets: A Synthesis of the Scientific Research on Adolescent Development:* [Minneapolis: Search Institute, 1999].)

FIGURE 2.5

Youth Who Report Experiencing the Commitment-to-Learning Assets

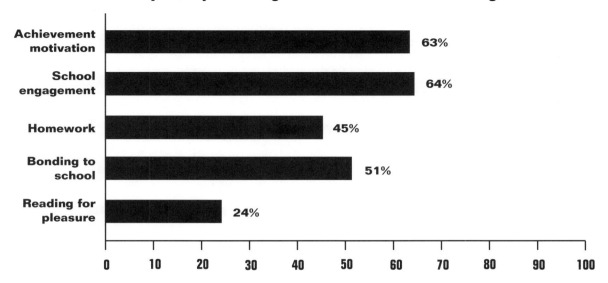

TABLE 2.5

Youth Who Report Experiencing the Commitment-to-Learning Assets, by Grade and Gender (in %)

ASSET		ALL	GRADE						
			6	7	8	9	10	11	12
21. Achievement motivation	All	63	70	66	61	63	62	63	62
	Females	71	76	72	67	69	70	72	73
	Males	56	65	59	54	56	53	53	51
22. School engagement	All	64	66	63	60	63	64	66	67
	Females	71	74	71	66	69	72	75	77
	Males	56	59	55	53	56	56	57	57
23. Homework	All	45	43	46	44	46	47	48	42
	Females	53	47	53	51	54	57	58	52
	Males	37	39	40	37	38	37	37	31
24. Bonding to school	All	51	64	54	46	51	50	49	49
	Females	56	70	60	51	55	54	53	53
	Males	46	58	49	40	47	45	44	44
25. Reading for pleasure	All	24	33	28	24	22	22	21	23
	Females	30	41	36	31	28	27	25	27
	Males	19	25	20	18	17	17	17	18

Positive Values

Positive values are important "internal compasses" that guide young people's priorities and choices. Although we seek to nurture many positive values, the asset framework focuses on six widely held values that help prevent high-risk behaviors and promote caring for others.

The first two positive-values assets are prosocial values that involve caring for others and the world. For the well-being of any society, young people need to learn how and when to suspend personal gain for the welfare of others. The four remaining positive-values assets focus more on personal character (they also reflect societal expectations, however). These values provide a basis for wise decision making.

Key findings

- Almost two-thirds of young people see themselves as having three of the positive values related to personal character: integrity (64 percent, asset #28), honesty (63 percent, asset #29), and responsibility (60 percent, asset #30).

- Less common are the values of caring for others and the world. Only 43 percent of youth affirm a commitment to helping others (asset #26, caring), and 45 percent affirm the importance of working for equality and social justice (asset

#27). Valuing restraint (asset #31) is also reported by less than half of the youth surveyed (42 percent).

- There is a gender gap in all six of these assets, with females being at least 10 percentage points higher than males on all of the positive-values assets.

- The percentage of youth reporting integrity increases from 6th to 12th grade. Reports of two assets (honesty and responsibility) appear to decline through 8th grade, then rise to close to the 6th-grade level. Reports of the remaining four assets in this category (caring, equality and social justice, integrity, and restraint) decline through middle and high school, with the steepest drop being the 50-point drop in the restraint asset.

Much attention has been paid in recent years to teaching young people positive values in school. While there is certainly a place for classroom learning about important values, it is important to remember that for these positive values to become more normative among young people, they must also be modeled by parents, grandparents, elders, neighbors, leaders, peers, mentors, and other role models. Furthermore, well-designed experiences of serving others can help to cement the value of caring for others.[3]

---

[3] See Alan Melcior, *Interim Report: National Evaluation of Learn and Serve American School and Community-based Programs* (Washington, DC: Corporation for National Service, 1997); Peter C. Scales, Dale A. Blyth, Thomas H. Berkas, and James C. Kielsmeier (1999), "The Effects of Service-Learning on Middle School Students' Social Responsibility and Academic Success" (manuscript submitted for publication).

FIGURE 2.6

Youth Who Report Experiencing the Positive-Values Assets

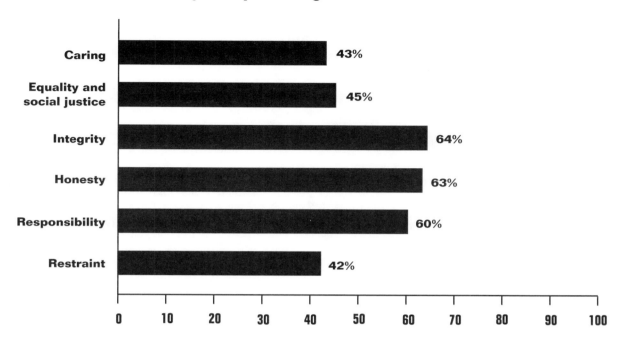

TABLE 2.6

Youth Who Report Experiencing the Positive-Values Assets, by Grade and Gender (in %)

ASSET		ALL	GRADE						
			6	7	8	9	10	11	12
26. Caring	All	43	56	49	42	40	40	39	42
	Females	54	64	59	52	52	52	52	55
	Males	32	48	40	31	29	27	27	30
27. Equality and social justice	All	45	59	52	45	43	41	39	40
	Females	57	66	62	56	55	54	52	53
	Males	33	52	42	34	30	28	25	26
28. Integrity	All	64	63	58	57	60	65	70	75
	Females	71	68	64	64	69	74	79	82
	Males	56	58	52	50	52	56	61	67
29. Honesty	All	63	73	65	59	59	60	62	67
	Females	69	78	71	65	65	67	68	74
	Males	56	69	60	53	52	53	56	59
30. Responsibility	All	60	65	59	55	57	60	64	67
	Females	65	70	64	60	61	65	69	72
	Males	55	60	54	50	53	54	58	62
31. Restraint	All	42	71	64	49	39	31	26	21
	Females	48	78	72	56	45	37	30	25
	Males	37	65	56	42	33	26	21	18

Social Competencies

Social competencies reflect the important personal skills young people need to negotiate through the maze of choices and challenges they face. These skills also lay a foundation for independence and competence as young adults. They give young people the tools they need to live out their values, beliefs, and priorities.

Two of the social-competencies assets (#32, planning and decision making, and #35, resistance skills) emphasize making personal choices. The other three (#33, interpersonal competence; #34, cultural competence; and #36, peaceful conflict resolution) focus on healthy interpersonal relationships.

Key findings

- Each of the five social competencies are experienced by less than half of the young people surveyed.

- There is a considerable gap between the reports of females and males in the social competencies, with females being more likely to report all of the social-competencies assets. The gap is 34 percentage points on interpersonal competence,

25 percentage points on peaceful conflict resolution, and 17 percentage points on cultural competence. Females report higher levels of the other assets in this category as well, though the differences are not as dramatic.

- While we might expect social competencies to increase through adolescence, reports of three of the five assets (cultural competence, resistance skills, and peaceful conflict resolution) decline between 6th and 12th grade. Reports of the other two dip slightly in 8th and 9th grades, but return to 6th-grade levels by high school graduation.

The gap in social-competencies assets between females and males is particularly salient given that young males are disproportionately the perpetrators of violence in schools and communities. While many factors contribute to this disturbing reality, a significant influence may be that our society has not been teaching boys how to relate with others without resorting to power, force, and violence to get their way. In addition, many of the heroes and role models for boys in popular culture model violence as a way of solving problems or interacting with others.

FIGURE 2.7

Youth Who Report Experiencing the Social-Competencies Assets

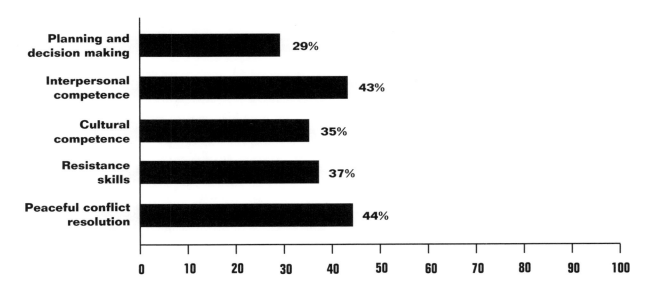

FIGURE 2.7

Youth Who Report Experiencing the Social-Competencies Assets, by Grade and Gender (in %)

ASSET		ALL	GRADE						
			6	7	8	9	10	11	12
32. Planning and decision making	All	29	31	28	26	26	28	31	33
	Females	33	36	33	30	29	32	35	38
	Males	25	26	24	23	23	23	26	28
33. Interpersonal competence	All	43	47	44	41	42	43	44	46
	Females	60	60	60	58	60	60	61	63
	Males	26	33	29	24	23	25	27	29
34. Cultural competence	All	35	41	39	36	36	33	31	29
	Females	43	48	46	45	45	42	39	38
	Males	26	34	32	27	26	23	23	21
35. Resistance skills	All	37	49	45	37	34	32	32	35
	Females	42	55	51	41	38	36	37	41
	Males	32	43	40	32	31	28	27	29
36. Peaceful conflict resolution	All	44	54	47	40	42	41	42	43
	Females	56	67	61	52	53	54	55	56
	Males	31	40	4	28	31	28	28	30

Positive Identity

The positive-identity assets focus on young people's view of themselves—their own sense of power, purpose, worth, and promise. Without these assets, young people risk feeling powerless and without a sense of initiative and purpose. These assets may be particularly important for young people whom the dominant culture identifies as "different," whether that difference has to do with gender, skin color, spiritual beliefs, sexual orientation, size and shape, or any number of other possibilities.

Key findings

- Two of the positive-identity assets (asset #39, sense of purpose, and asset #40, positive view of personal future) are reported by more than half of the youth surveyed. A positive view of personal future has the highest percentage of any of the 40 assets.

- Unlike other categories of assets, reports of the positive-identity assets remain relatively stable or actually increase from 6th to 12th grade. Personal power (asset #37) climbs by 16 percentage points across the grade span. One might expect reports of the positive-identity assets to increase over the course of adolescence because adolescence is a time in which a great deal of this development takes place.

- While gender differences are small for two of the four positive-identity assets (personal power and positive view of personal future), males are more likely than females to report experiencing the other two assets: self-esteem (#38) and sense of purpose (#39).

- Most young people (70 percent) are optimistic about their future. In the face of the challenges many young people face, this perspective may say something about the human spirit or about teenage idealism. This finding may also reflect a measurement issue, because our measure asks only about a belief in having "a good life" as an adult. It is therefore an incomplete examination of beliefs about different aspects of the future.

The process of internalizing a sense of self is one of the central tasks of adolescence. Some young people shape their identity in passive ways, simply accepting the roles and self-images imposed on them by others—a process that can lead to self-doubt and uncertainty. When young people are encouraged to actively explore who they are and are becoming, they are more likely to be self-assured and have a sense of mastery. These four assets remind us of the importance of focusing intentionally and actively on nurturing a positive identity.[4]

---

[4] See, e.g., E. H. Erikson, *Identity: Youth and Crisis* (New York: Norton, 1968).

FIGURE 2.8

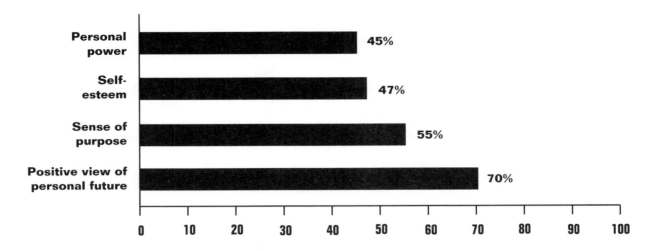

Youth Who Report Experiencing the Positive-Identity Assets

FIGURE 2.8

Youth Who Report Experiencing the Positive-Identity Assets, by Grade and Gender (in %)

ASSET		ALL	GRADE						
			6	7	8	9	10	11	12
37. Personal power	All	45	40	40	41	44	47	51	56
	Females	46	40	42	41	45	46	51	56
	Males	45	40	39	40	43	41	52	55
38. Self-esteem	All	47	52	48	45	44	44	48	50
	Females	40	49	43	38	37	36	40	44
	Males	54	55	53	52	52	52	55	56
39. Sense of purpose	All	55	57	55	53	53	52	56	60
	Females	50	55	52	47	47	45	51	57
	Males	60	58	58	59	59	60	61	62
40. Positive view of personal future	All	70	72	70	69	69	69	71	74
	Females	71	72	70	69	69	69	72	75
	Males	70	72	69	69	69	70	70	73

Putting the Pieces Together

Each of the developmental assets matters. Each contributes to healthy development. However, the true power of asset building is cumulative in that these 40 assets build on and enrich each other. As we will see in Chapter 5, increasing the number of assets young people experience can have a profound impact on their well-being.

But the gap between the ideal and the real is wide in every community we have studied. Throughout this chapter, we have highlighted patterns of the assets in each category. When we look at specific assets, however, we discover that far too many of them are lacking. Figure 2.9 shows all 40 assets in descending order based on the percentages of youth who report experiencing them. Of the 40 assets, 27 are experienced by half or less of the young people surveyed.

FIGURE 2.9

Youth Who Report Experiencing Each of 40 Assets, Total Sample, in Descending Order

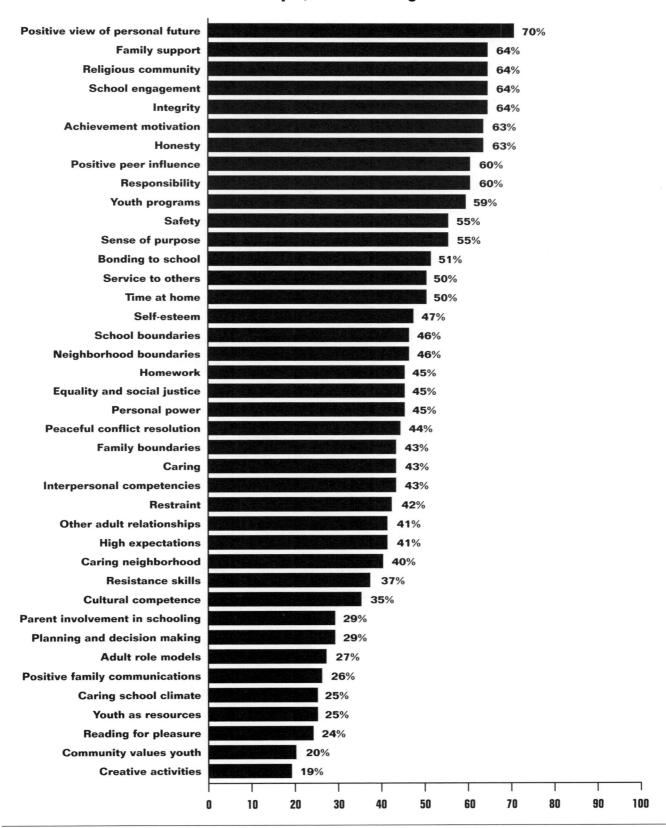

Asset	Percent
Positive view of personal future	70%
Family support	64%
Religious community	64%
School engagement	64%
Integrity	64%
Achievement motivation	63%
Honesty	63%
Positive peer influence	60%
Responsibility	60%
Youth programs	59%
Safety	55%
Sense of purpose	55%
Bonding to school	51%
Service to others	50%
Time at home	50%
Self-esteem	47%
School boundaries	46%
Neighborhood boundaries	46%
Homework	45%
Equality and social justice	45%
Personal power	45%
Peaceful conflict resolution	44%
Family boundaries	43%
Caring	43%
Interpersonal competencies	43%
Restraint	42%
Other adult relationships	41%
High expectations	41%
Caring neighborhood	40%
Resistance skills	37%
Cultural competence	35%
Parent involvement in schooling	29%
Planning and decision making	29%
Adult role models	27%
Positive family communications	26%
Caring school climate	25%
Youth as resources	25%
Reading for pleasure	24%
Community values youth	20%
Creative activities	19%

Overall Levels of Developmental Assets

In communities all across the country, the state of developmental assets is too fragile. Ideally, youth will experience almost all of these 40 developmental assets. However, an examination of our sample of youth shows how far we have to go.

Average level of assets

Youth report having, on average, 18 of the 40 assets. Although we see some variation across communities and in different subgroups of youth (as shown on the pages that follow), the variation does not detract from the central message: The vast majority of youth—regardless of age, gender, race/ethnicity, family composition, family income level, and community size—experience far too few of these 40 developmental assets. This rather sobering finding would likely be even lower if the school-based studies also included those youth who had dropped out of school.

Youth with different levels of assets

Another way to view the current levels of assets is to divide the sample into those who experience different levels of assets: 0-10 assets, 11-20 assets, 21-30 assets, and 31-40 assets. As shown in Figure 2.10, almost two-thirds (63 percent) of the young people surveyed experience half or less of the 40 assets. Furthermore, only 8 percent of youth report experiencing 31 or more of the assets—a level that we consider an appropriate goal for all young people.

Comparisons by gender group show that, while females report experiencing more assets than males do, less than half (45 percent) of females experience more than half of the assets. Only 30 percent of males experience more than half of the assets.

Comparisons of levels across grades add a different perspective (Table 2.9). Among 6th graders, 15 percent report having a high level of assets (31 or more). However, among 12th graders, just 4 percent are asset-rich youth, with the greatest percentage change in reporting occurring by 8th grade. In short, far too many young people complete high school without having built a solid foundation for life.

TABLE 2.9

Youth Reporting Each Level of Assets, by Grade (in %)

Grade	YOUTH WITH EACH LEVEL OF ASSETS			
	0-10 Assets	11-20 Assets	21-30 Assets	31-40 Assets
6	10	35	40	15
7	15	38	35	12
8	22	41	29	8
9	22	43	28	7
10	23	45	27	5
11	22	47	27	5
12	19	49	28	4

FIGURE 2.10

Youth Who Report Experiencing Each Level of Assets, Overall and by Gender

TOTAL SAMPLE

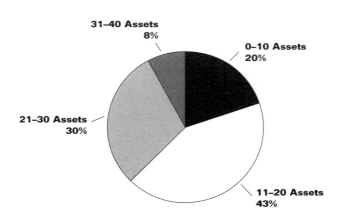

31–40 Assets
8%

0–10 Assets
20%

21–30 Assets
30%

11–20 Assets
43%

FEMALES

MALES

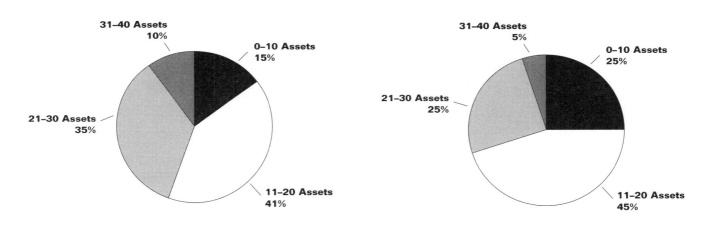

FEMALES

31–40 Assets
10%

0–10 Assets
15%

21–30 Assets
35%

11–20 Assets
41%

MALES

31–40 Assets
5%

0–10 Assets
25%

21–30 Assets
25%

11–20 Assets
45%

NOTE: Numbers may not add to 100% due to rounding.

Levels of Assets in Specific Subgroups of Youth ——

To this point, we have focused primarily on the overall patterns of assets among all youth. When we look at specific subgroups of youth, we begin to see some differences in their experiences of assets, though none of the subgroups we have studied has a dramatically different asset profile. (Appendix A contains a detailed description of the differences in the individual assets by various group differences: race/ethnicity, community size, maternal education, and family composition.)

Age

Theoretically, it would be desirable for assets to increase between 6th and 12th grade. There is some evidence, however, that the average number of assets declines across this age span, from 21.5 in grade 6 to 17.2 in grade 12. (See Figure 2.11.)

On one level, a decline in assets may seem inevitable, if not desirable, as young people mature and become more independent. But while some assets may become less essential across time (for example, family boundaries change as independence grows), there is no reason for most of the assets to become less important. For example, positive role models remain significant for all ages. In addition, we would hope the overall level of assets would increase as young people internalize the internal assets. In reality, the overall level of external assets decreases from 6th to 12th grade, but the level of internal assets remains essentially unchanged.

It is important to note that this research is cross-sectional, not longitudinal. That is, these percentages reflect responses of youth across grade levels who were all surveyed at about the same time; they do not show whether or how levels of assets for one young person or one group may change across time. A series of longitudinal studies begun in 1998 will shed additional light on this issue.

FIGURE 2.11 ————

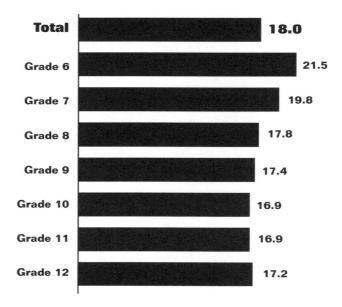

Average Number of Assets, by Grade

Total	18.0
Grade 6	21.5
Grade 7	19.8
Grade 8	17.8
Grade 9	17.4
Grade 10	16.9
Grade 11	16.9
Grade 12	17.2

Gender

Females report an average of about three more assets than males (19.5 vs. 16.5), as shown in Figure 2.12. This pattern holds in each grade between 6 and 12. That is, in every grade, females report having more assets than males do. Our research has shown that, although the gender differences may not be large, they appear to be rather pervasive, suggesting "differences in the contextual experiences of boys and girls over the adolescent period."[5]

FIGURE 2.12

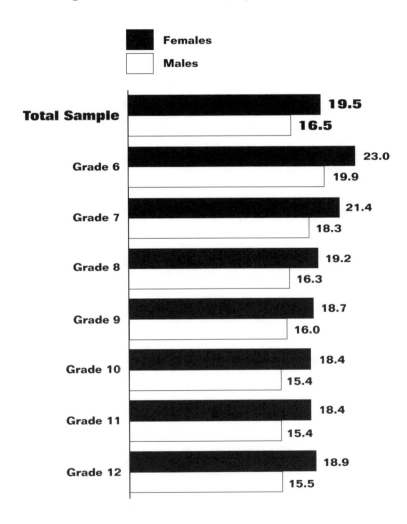

Average Number of Assets, by Gender and Grade

- ■ Females
- □ Males

	Females	Males
Total Sample	19.5	16.5
Grade 6	23.0	19.9
Grade 7	21.4	18.3
Grade 8	19.2	16.3
Grade 9	18.7	16.0
Grade 10	18.4	15.4
Grade 11	18.4	15.4
Grade 12	18.9	15.5

[5] N. Leffert, P. L. Benson, P. C. Scales, A. R. Sharma, D. R. Drake, and D. A. Blyth, "Developmental Assets: Measurement and Prediction of Risk Behaviors among Adolescents," *Applied Developmental Science, 2* (1998), 209-230. This article contains a complete description of the gender and age differences within this aggregate sample.

Race/Ethnicity

Small variations in the average number of assets can be seen as a function of race/ethnicity. Asian American, African American, and White youth in our large sample appear to have similar numbers of assets (18.4, 18.7, and 18.1, respectively). American Indian youth average fewer assets (15.7) than other subgroups, as do youth who describe themselves as multiracial (16.9). (See Figure 2.13.)

We urge caution in generalizing from these data on differences among racial/ethnic groups. As noted in Chapter 1, our aggregate sample underrepresents young people of color and those from large cities, where a disproportionate percentage of people of color live. Further research is needed to either confirm or challenge the differences and similarities seen in this sample.

Family composition

Youth in two-parent families average several more assets than youth in single-parent families. Those who spend part of their time with their father and part with their mother do slightly better than those who live only with one parent. Young people who live only with their father report lower average asset levels than those who live only with their mother.

Maternal education

Researchers sometimes use maternal education as an approximate measure of family income, because children whose mothers have less education are more likely to be poor.[6] We find that maternal education makes a difference in young people's experience of assets. As the mother's education level rises, so does the average number of assets. This trend suggests that young people living in poverty are likely to experience fewer assets than youth from wealthier families (or those with higher maternal education). However, even youth whose mothers have gone to graduate school only have 20.4 of the 40 assets.

Type of community

Contrary to common expectations, assets are no more common in small towns than in larger cities. Youth living in towns with populations under 2,500 average 17.6 assets. Youth in cities larger than 250,000 average 17.9. (Additional research in major cities is needed to determine whether this finding is generalizable.) However, as can be seen in Appendix A, young people who live on reservations may be less likely to experience many of the individual assets than young people in other types of communities.

Summary

Many factors influence young people's levels of assets. Age and gender have a greater effect than the other variables examined. Yet, amid the subtle differences, the overall pattern remains strong: All groups of youth in all types of settings and places possess too few of the developmental assets.

While these data may suggest that certain groups of young people (for example, females, African American youth, youth in two-parent families, those whose families have a higher socioeconomic status, and those who live in small cities) report having relatively higher levels of assets, the asset foundation is fragile for all groups of youth (see Appendixes A-D for detailed descriptions of these differences). All youth would benefit from having more assets in their lives.

---

[6] Using maternal education as a proxy for socioeconomic status has been validated in a number of studies. See, e.g., K. L. Glasgow, S. M. Dornbusch, L. Troyer, L. Steinberg, and P. L. Ritter, "Parenting Styles, Adolescents' Attributions, and Educational Outcomes in Nine Heterogeneous High Schools," *Child Development, 68* (1997), 507-529.

FIGURE 2.13

Average Number of Assets, by Selected Other Demographic Variables

RACE/ETHNICITY

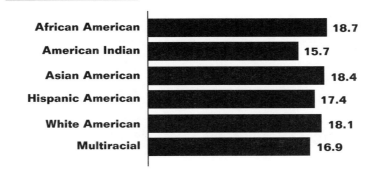

African American	18.7
American Indian	15.7
Asian American	18.4
Hispanic American	17.4
White American	18.1
Multiracial	16.9

FAMILY COMPOSITION

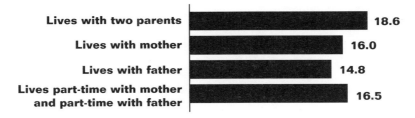

Lives with two parents	18.6
Lives with mother	16.0
Lives with father	14.8
Lives part-time with mother and part-time with father	16.5

LEVEL OF MOTHER'S EDUCATION

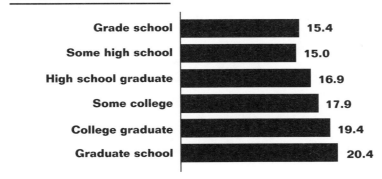

Grade school	15.4
Some high school	15.0
High school graduate	16.9
Some college	17.9
College graduate	19.4
Graduate school	20.4

TYPE OF COMMUNITY

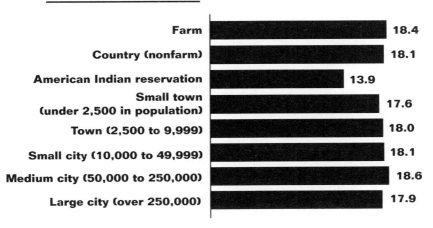

Farm	18.4
Country (nonfarm)	18.1
American Indian reservation	13.9
Small town (under 2,500 in population)	17.6
Town (2,500 to 9,999)	18.0
Small city (10,000 to 49,999)	18.1
Medium city (50,000 to 250,000)	18.6
Large city (over 250,000)	17.9

The Challenge

This portrait of developmental assets is unsettling. Regardless of gender, cultural background, town size, or geographical location, today's young people typically:

- Receive too little support through sustained and positive intergenerational relationships;

- Lack opportunities for leadership and involvement;

- Disengage from youth-serving programs in the community;

- Experience inconsistent or unarticulated boundaries;

- Feel disconnected from and unvalued by their community; and

- Miss the formation of social competencies and positive values.

As long as these patterns continue, we will see too many young people who are susceptible to risky behaviors and negative pressure, drawn to undesirable sources of belonging (e.g., gangs), and ill-equipped to become the next generation of parents, workers, leaders, and citizens.

3

Deficits and Risks
in Young People's Lives

On average, young people experience fewer than half of the 40 developmental assets. This disturbing piece of the picture of adolescent development suggests that young people do not have the resources and strengths they need to thrive. Equally disturbing are the realities surrounding many of the risks young people face. This chapter focuses on two types of challenges:

- **Developmental deficits,** which are liabilities that may be dangerous by themselves (such as being a victim of violence) and that may also increase the odds that a young person will engage in risky behaviors. While many such deficits could be named, we measure and report on five developmental deficits.

- **High-risk behavior patterns,** which are patterns of destructive behavior that potentially limit

psychological, physical, or economic health and well-being during adolescence and adulthood. This chapter focuses on 10 such high-risk behavior patterns.

As we will see in this chapter, far too many youth are facing far too many challenges and dangers. And, as we noted earlier, our sample of youth, though large, overrepresents White youth from smaller towns and cities, and youth whose parents have a higher-than-average level of education. Furthermore, since surveys are completed in schools, the sample does not include some of the most vulnerable youth: those who have dropped out of school. Thus, the findings presented in this chapter likely underestimate the levels of both deficits and high-risk behaviors and do not adequately capture the depth of these problems for all types of young people in our society.

Defining Developmental Deficits

Developmental deficits are "negative influences or realities in young people's lives that make it more difficult for them to develop in healthy, caring, and productive ways. They are liabilities that may not do permanent harm but make harm more possible."[1] These developmental challenges include highly traumatic experiences, such as sexual abuse, family violence, parental addiction, neglect, poverty, and experiencing the horrors of war. Other less traumatic experiences that are becoming commonplace can also interfere with healthy development. Among these are spending too much time alone, overexposure to television, and attending parties where many or all youth consume alcohol.

Not all of these deficits can be measured effectively or completely with a self-report survey such as the one used to gather the information in this report. We measure five developmental deficits (shown in Table 3.1), which are discussed briefly here.

Alone at home

While spending time at home is considered an asset (#20), spending too much time alone at home—without supervision—is not. Extensive research has shown the dangers associated with unstructured, unsupervised time, particularly in the after-school hours—a time when adolescents are most likely to be victims and perpetrators of crime,[2] and when they are more likely to engage in other risky behaviors.[3]

TV overexposure

The evidence is strong that watching too much television is harmful to young people. Not only can it expose them to excessive violence, inappropriate levels of explicit sexual activity for their age level, and other potentially harmful messages, but overexposure to TV also means that they are not using that time for constructive, stimulating activities such as recreation, volunteer work, homework, and the arts.[4]

Physical abuse

Being physically abused increases the chances that young people's physical and emotional health may be at risk, that they will do less well at school, and that they will engage in high-risk behaviors.[5] Although infants less than a year old are twice as likely as 16- to 18-year-olds to be physically abused,[6] and maltreatment of 6- to 11-year-olds has increased the most

[1] Peter L. Benson, *All Kids Are Our Kids: What Communities Must Do to Raise Caring and Responsible Children and Adolescents* (San Francisco: Jossey-Bass, 1997), 14.

[2] Howard N. Snyder, Melissa Sickmund, and Eileen Poe-Yamagata, *Juvenile Offenders and Victims: 1996 Update on Violence* (Washington, DC: U.S. Department of Justice, Office of Juvenile Justice and Delinquency Prevention, 1996).

[3] Carnegie Council on Adolescent Development, *A Matter of Time: Risk and Opportunity in the Nonschool Hours* (New York: Carnegie Corporation of New York, 1992); and Reginald M. Clark, *Critical Factors in Why Disadvantaged Students Succeed or Fail in School* (Washington, DC: Academy for Educational Development, 1988).

[4] For more on the impact of television on young people, see the special issue, "Television and Teens: Health Implications," *Journal of Adolescent Health Care, 11* (1990).

[5] Diana J. English, "The Extent and Consequences of Child Maltreatment," *Future of Children, 8*, no. 1 (Spring 1998), 39-53.

[6] *Ibid.*

since 1986,[7] *young* adolescents ages 12 to 14 have in recent years been the most likely age-group to be abused.[8]

Physical abuse is only one dimension of the maltreatment of children and youth. According to the U.S. Department of Justice, the greatest proportion of juveniles (from birth through age 18) who are victims of maltreatment suffer from neglect (50 percent), followed by physical abuse (24 percent), sexual abuse (15 percent), emotional maltreatment (5 percent), medical neglect (2 percent), or other types of maltreatment (15 percent).[9] The deficit assesses only the general report of "one or more incidents of physical abuse in lifetime" and therefore only gives a sense of the larger area of maltreatment young people may face, not specific types of abuse.

Victim of violence

While there is reason to worry about young people engaging in acts of violence, young people may be more likely to be victims of violence than to be perpetrators. Furthermore, being victimized not only brings physical and emotional harm, it also increases the chances that those youth will in turn be violent toward others.[10] The violent victimization rate for teenagers is twice as high as for any other age-group. With the exception of rape (for which adolescent females are the most frequent victims), adolescent males, especially African Americans, have the highest violent victimization rates of all.[11]

Drinking parties

Parties where young people are drinking directly expose young people to two serious risks: problem alcohol use, and drinking and driving. Substantial proportions of young people put themselves and others at risk of injury because of alcohol use. According to the Centers for Disease Control and Prevention's *Youth Risk Behavior Surveillance* survey, 37 percent of 9th to 12th graders rode in the past year with a driver who had been drinking, and 17 percent said they personally drove after drinking.[12] In addition, young people are more likely to engage in sexual intercourse, especially unprotected and/or forced intercourse, if they have been drinking.[13]

---

[7] "Child Abuse and Neglect National Incidence Study," *Washington Social Legislation Bulletin, 34* (September 23, 1996), 165-168.

[8] Department of Health and Human Services, *Study Findings: Study of National Incidence and Prevalence of Child Abuse and Neglect: 1988* (Washington, DC: Department of Health and Human Services, 1988).

[9] Snyder et al., *Juvenile Offenders and Victims: 1996 Update on Violence.*

[10] R. G. Slaby, "Violence: Its Prevalence and Some Responses," in *Resilient Youth in a Violent World: Edited Transcripts of a 1994 Summer Program of the Harvard Collaborative for School Counseling and Support Services* (Cambridge, MA: Harvard University, Graduate School of Education, 1995), 25-30; and R. L. Simons, K.-H. Lin, and L. C. Gordon, "Socialization in the Family of Origin and Male Dating Violence: A Prospective Study," *Journal of Marriage and the Family, 60,* no. 2 (1998), 467-478.

[11] National Crime Prevention Council, *How Communities Can Bring Up Youth Free from Fear and Violence* (Washington, DC: National Crime Prevention Council, 1995).

[12] L. Kann et al., *Youth Risk Behavior Surveillance—United States, 1997.* MMWR Surveillance Summaries, August 14, 1998/47(SS-3); 1-89.

[13] B. C. Miller, "Risk Factors for Nonmarital Childbearing," in *Report to Congress on Out-of-Wedlock Childbearing,* Pub. No. PHS-95-1257 (Washington, DC: Department of Health and Human Services, 1995), 217-227.

Why poverty is not measured as a deficit

We do not directly measure one of the most pervasive deficits in many young people's lives: poverty. We know from government research that one in five children under age 18 lives in poverty.[14] And there is extensive research showing that poverty interferes with young people's growth and development, putting them at greater risk of choosing harmful behaviors and limiting their options for the future.[15]

We do not include poverty as a deficit because we cannot directly examine its impact through our self-report survey method. Young people tend not to be accurate reporters of family income. In addition, because all the students in our sample were surveyed anonymously, no identification numbers or other means of linking their responses to other secondary sources of information that measure poverty status (e.g., receiving free or reduced-cost lunches) were used.

We do, however, ask youth to report on their mother's education, which is widely considered to be an adequate proxy variable for family socioeconomic status. Examining young people's experiences in light of this variable shows that, indeed, poverty does act as a deficit, making it less likely for young people to experience assets, more likely to engage in high-risk behaviors, and less likely to experience thriving indicators. (See the Appendixes for detailed data by maternal education.)

Of course, much more research is needed—including studies in impoverished neighborhoods and communities—to document with confidence the connections between socioeconomic status and developmental assets. Several studies are under way that will add to our understanding of these issues.

[14] U.S. Bureau of the Census, *Current Population Reports: Poverty in the United States 1995* (Washington, DC: U.S. Bureau of the Census, 1997).

[15] J. Brooks-Gunn, G. J. Duncan, P. K. Klebanov, and N. Sealand, "Do Neighborhoods Influence Child and Adolescent Development?" (1993), *American Journal of Sociology, 99*, 353-395.

TABLE 3.1

Developmental Deficits

DEFICIT	DEFINITION
Alone at home	Spends two hours or more per school day alone at home.
TV overexposure	Watches television or videos three or more hours per school day.
Physical abuse	Reports one or more incidents of physical abuse in lifetime.
Victim of violence	Reports being a victim of violence one or more times in the past two years.
Drinking parties	Reports attending one or more parties in the past year "where other kids your age were drinking."

For a list of items used to measure each deficit, see Table B.2 in Appendix B.

Young People's Experiences of Developmental Deficits

Figure 3.1 shows the percentages of young people who report each of the five deficits, and Table 3.2 shows experiences of deficits by gender within grade.

Key findings

- Two of the deficits are experienced by about half of the youth surveyed: attending drinking parties (51 percent) and being home alone (48 percent).

- Females and males are equally likely to report attending parties where drinking takes place and spending two or more hours per school day alone at home. Males report more overexposure to television and more often being victims of violence; females report more physical abuse than males do.

- The percentage of youth who report that they go to parties where other youth are drinking increases steadily across the age span, with especially large jumps in each grade between 7th and 10th grade. By 9th grade, a majority of adolescents go to parties where there is drinking. By the 12th grade, four out of five youth attend such parties.

- Approximately one-third of the young people surveyed watch three or more hours of television on school days. The percentage climbs slightly from 6th to 8th grade, then declines steadily to 23 percent in 12th grade. This decline is likely associated with increased independence and new social activities made possible by having a driver's license.

- The percentage of young people who report being physically abused increases slightly throughout middle school, then declines through high school.

- As with overexposure to television and physical abuse, the percentage of youth who report being victims of violence increases slightly through middle school, then declines through high school. (The same pattern of increasing through middle school and declining through high school occurs with young people's reports of being perpetrators of violence, as we will see later in this chapter when discussing high-risk behaviors.)

FIGURE 3.1

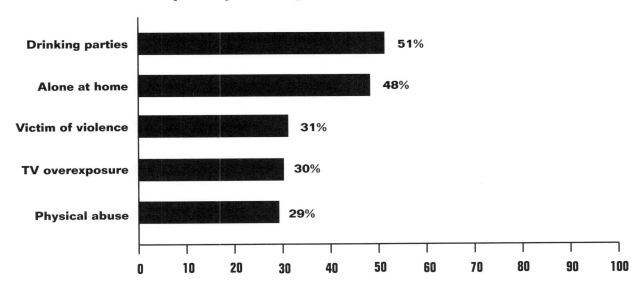

Youth Who Report Experiencing Each Deficit, in Descending Order

TABLE 3.2

Youth Who Report Experiencing Each Deficit, in Descending Order and by Grade and Gender (in %)

DEFICITS		ALL	GRADE						
			6	7	8	9	10	11	12
Drinking parties	**All**	**51**	**14**	**23**	**41**	**54**	**66**	**75**	**80**
	Females	51	12	22	42	55	67	74	78
	Males	51	15	24	40	52	65	76	82
Alone at home	**All**	**48**	**41**	**44**	**48**	**50**	**50**	**50**	**50**
	Females	49	40	44	49	51	51	51	51
	Males	48	42	45	48	49	49	49	50
Victim of violence	**All**	**31**	**31**	**32**	**34**	**34**	**31**	**27**	**24**
	Females	27	25	26	29	30	28	26	23
	Males	34	37	38	38	37	34	29	26
TV overexposure	**All**	**30**	**32**	**35**	**36**	**32**	**28**	**24**	**23**
	Females	27	30	31	33	28	24	21	20
	Males	34	35	39	40	36	33	27	25
Physical abuse	**All**	**29**	**30**	**31**	**32**	**31**	**29**	**26**	**24**
	Females	31	29	30	34	33	32	29	25
	Males	27	32	31	31	29	26	23	23

Number of Deficits Young People Experience

Few youth are free of the negative influences described by these deficits. Indeed, only 15 percent of youth experience none of the five measured deficits (Figure 3.2). Furthermore, 3 percent experience all five of these deficits, suggesting that these young people face formidable challenges in growing up.

As Table 3.3 shows, the situation gets worse as youth get older. Most of the increase in average number of deficits across ages may be attributed to the increased independence that makes older youth more likely to attend parties where young people are drinking (the

deficit with the greatest increase from 6th to 12th grades).

These findings also reemphasize that young people do not experience deficits in isolation of each other. Rather, young people most often face a constellation of challenges at the same time, making it difficult for narrowly defined interventions to have much impact, since one deficit often feeds and reinforces another. Realities such as these suggest that we must find appropriate ways to help young people gain independence while protecting them from risky situations.

FIGURE 3.2

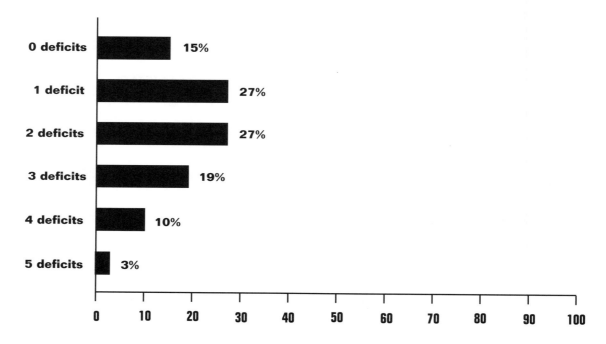

Youth Who Report Experiencing Different Levels of Deficits

TABLE 3.3

Youth Who Report Experiencing Each Level of Deficits, by Grade and Gender (in %)

NUMBER OF DEFICITS		ALL	GRADE						
			6	7	8	9	10	11	12
0	All	15	26	23	17	13	11	9	7
	Females	16	31	26	19	14	12	9	8
	Males	13	22	19	15	13	11	8	7
1	All	27	29	28	25	25	26	28	29
	Females	27	29	28	25	25	27	29	31
	Males	26	29	27	25	25	25	28	28
2	All	27	24	25	25	27	28	30	32
	Females	26	22	23	25	27	29	29	32
	Males	28	26	27	25	28	29	31	32
3	All	19	14	15	19	20	21	20	21
	Females	18	13	14	18	19	20	19	19
	Males	20	15	16	21	20	22	21	22
4	All	10	6	8	10	11	11	10	9
	Females	10	5	7	10	12	11	10	9
	Males	9	6	9	10	11	11	9	9
5	All	3	1	2	3	3	3	3	2
	Females	3	1	2	3	3	3	3	2
	Males	3	2	3	4	4	3	3	2

Average Levels of Deficits

Another way to understand the impact of deficits is to determine the average number of deficits young people report, as shown in Figure 3.3.

Key findings

- The average young person surveyed experiences 1.9 of the 5 deficits.

- The average number of the 5 deficits jumps the most across the middle school years, between 6th and 8th grade, from 1.5 to 1.9. From 9th through 12th grade, the number remains stable.

- Males experience a slightly higher average number of deficits than females. Although the over- all levels are quite close, females tend to experience different deficits than do males, as noted earlier.

Thus, the average young person surveyed reports experiencing 2 of the 5 developmental deficits during high school. While young people have some control over several of these deficits (especially attending drinking parties, TV overexposure, and, in some cases, youth-on-youth violence), families and communities must bear a share of the responsibility for the fact that so many young people must contend with these deficits. Unless we find ways to make these experiences less common, far too many young people will struggle to beat the odds that we have helped place against them.

FIGURE 3.3

Average Number of Five Deficits, by Gender and Grade

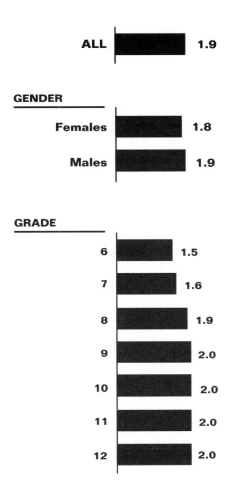

Deficits in Specific Subgroups of Youth

Approximately 85 percent of the youth surveyed experience at least one of the five deficits. Clearly, then, no group of young people is immune from them. While there certainly are differences in deficit levels in different populations of youth, it is important to keep a basic finding in mind: The majority of youth—regardless of race/ethnicity, family composition, type of community—experience the challenges of having one or more of these deficits in their lives.

At the same time, unique patterns and challenges emerge when we look at specific groups of young people. In other words, some youth are more likely to experience deficits than others. Table 3.4 shows the average number of deficits for young people as a function of various differences and the percentages of each group that experience different levels of deficits. (For the more detailed findings on specific deficits in each subgroup, see Appendix B.)

Race/Ethnicity

Across different races, Asian American youth are somewhat less likely to report experiencing the deficits, except for watching too much television, a deficit least common among White American youth. Hispanic American youth are the most likely to attend parties where youth are drinking (64 percent), and African American youth the most likely to watch too much television (75 percent).

Multiracial (42 percent) and American Indian (35 percent) students report experiencing physical abuse at a higher percentage than the average (29 percent). These two groups also are more likely to have been victims of violence (45 percent and 38 percent, respectively) compared to the average student (31 percent). White,

Hispanic, and African American youth are about equally likely to have been victims of violence (about 30 percent), with Asian American youth being least likely to have been victims of violence (25 percent).

Type of community

Community size makes less difference in the average number of deficits than might be expected. The clearest pattern is that American Indian youth living on reservations experience the highest average number of deficits. In general, youth who live in the country or on farms experience the lowest average number of the deficits.

Maternal education

As with family composition, mother's education (which we use as an indicator of the family's socioeconomic status) plays an important role in affecting the chances that youth have deficits. In general, youth whose mothers have only some high school education have the highest average number of deficits, and those whose mothers graduated from college have the least.

Family composition

There is a difference in the percentages of youth who experience each level of deficits, depending on family composition. This difference is apparent in the average number of deficits experienced by youth in two-parent families: 1.8, which is lower than the average number for any other type of family, as shown in Table 3.4.

TABLE 3.4

Average Number of Five Deficits and Percentage of Youth Who Report Experiencing Each Level of Deficits, by Selected Demographic Variables

	Average Number of Deficits	PERCENTAGE EXPERIENCING EACH LEVEL OF DEFICITS					
		0 Deficits	1 Deficit	2 Deficits	3 Deficits	4 Deficits	5 Deficits
All	**1.9**	**15**	**27**	**27**	**19**	**10**	**3**
Gender							
Female	1.8	16	27	26	18	10	3
Male	1.9	13	26	28	20	9	3
Grade							
6	1.5	26	29	24	14	6	1
7	1.6	23	28	25	15	8	2
8	1.9	17	25	25	19	10	3
9	2.0	13	25	27	20	11	3
10	2.0	11	26	28	21	11	3
11	2.0	9	28	30	20	10	3
12	2.0	7	29	32	21	9	2
Race/Ethnicity							
African American	2.3	8	20	30	25	12	4
American Indian	2.2	11	23	26	23	13	5
Asian American	1.8	20	26	26	17	8	2
Hispanic American	2.1	11	24	27	23	11	4
White American	1.9	15	27	27	18	9	3
Multiracial	2.3	9	21	26	23	15	6
Type of Community							
Farm	1.8	17	29	27	17	8	2
Country	1.8	16	28	27	18	9	3
Reservation	2.4	7	19	27	24	15	7
Small town	2.0	14	26	27	20	10	3
Town	1.9	14	27	27	19	10	3
Small city	1.9	14	27	28	19	9	3
City	1.9	15	26	28	19	10	2
Large city	2.1	14	22	27	21	12	4
Maternal Education							
Grade school	2.1	14	23	26	21	11	5
Some high school	2.3	10	21	26	23	15	5
High school graduate	1.9	13	27	28	20	10	3
Some college	2.0	13	26	28	20	10	3
College graduate	1.8	17	29	27	17	8	2
Graduate school	1.8	17	27	27	18	9	3
Don't know	1.9	17	25	27	19	10	4
Family Composition							
Live with two parents	1.8	17	28	27	18	8	2
Live with mother	2.3	9	21	29	23	14	4
Live with father	2.4	7	19	30	23	15	5
Live part-time with each parent	2.2	10	23	26	22	14	5

Defining Patterns of High-Risk Behaviors

Risky behaviors have become—at least in popular culture—emblematic of adolescence; adults seem to *expect* young people to engage in them. This expectation grows in part out of mixed messages to youth, inaccurate beliefs that "everybody's doing it," and false notions that adolescence is, by definition, a time of conflict and rebellion. At the same time, some experimentation in risky activities is part of normal adolescent development—an outgrowth of the experimentation with values and behaviors that comes with identity formation.

Like other studies, our data show that, indeed, most young people (81 percent) have engaged in some kind of risky behavior by the time they finish high school. While some of this experimentation can be dangerous and potentially life-changing (such as unprotected sexual intercourse) and some activities are illegal (such as using illicit drugs) or are widely considered unethical or immoral (such as acts of violence), many young people experiment without doing permanent harm or taking up a lifestyle of risky behaviors. For example, a young person may go gambling with friends or get drunk without experiencing serious long-term conse-

quences. Furthermore, a young person might choose to stop doing something negative because of new circumstances, beliefs, or other changes.

Because an individual incidence of risk taking may be developmentally normative and is most often correctable, we focus on the *high-risk behavior patterns* that indicate that youth are on more serious and persistently unhealthy or dangerous paths. For example, youth who report using tobacco just once in the past 30 days have the individual risk of tobacco use (since no use would be best for their health), but those who smoke *every day* are clearly at greater risk of health problems. Therefore, we define daily use as a *pattern* of risky behavior for tobacco.

Table 3.5 identifies and defines 10 patterns of high-risk behavior that we measure. (Items used to measure these behaviors are shown in Appendix C.) Many of the cutoff points are intentionally set at a very high level to avoid overdramatizing the extent of problems among youth and to emphasize that these patterns are dangerous and can have lifelong consequences for young people and society.

TABLE 3.5

Definitions of 10 High-Risk Behavior Patterns

HIGH-RISK BEHAVIOR PATTERN	DEFINITION
Problem alcohol use	Has used alcohol three or more times in the past 30 days or has gotten drunk once or more in the past two weeks.
Tobacco use	Smokes one or more cigarettes every day or frequently uses chewing tobacco.
Illicit drug use	Has used illicit drugs (such as marijuana, cocaine, LSD, PCP or angel dust, heroin or other narcotics, amphetamines) three or more times in the past 12 months.
Sexual intercourse	Has had sexual intercourse three or more times in lifetime.
Depression and suicide	Is frequently depressed and/or has attempted suicide.
Antisocial behavior	Has been involved in three or more incidents of shoplifting, trouble with police, or vandalism in the past 12 months.
Violence	Has engaged in three or more acts of fighting, hitting, injuring a person, carrying or using a weapon, or threatening physical harm in the past 12 months.
School problems	Has skipped school two or more days in the past four weeks and/or has below a C average.
Driving and alcohol	Has driven after drinking or ridden with a drinking driver three or more times in the past 12 months.
Gambling	Has gambled three or more times in the past 12 months.

For a list of items used to measure each high-risk behavior pattern, see Table C.2 in Appendix C.

Overall Involvement in High-Risk Behavior Patterns

Figure 3.4 and Table 3.6 show that considerable proportions of young people engage in these patterns of high-risk behavior. While none of the patterns is reported by a majority of 6th to 12th graders, some youth engage in every high-risk behavior pattern, with involvement generally higher among older youth. Large percentages of young people, therefore, are at risk of harming themselves and others, lessening their chances of being successful, and depriving their communities of their potential positive contributions.

Key findings

- Almost one in five youth reports engaging in one of the 10 high-risk behavior patterns. The most prevalent patterns are violence and problem alcohol use.

- By the end of the 8th grade, almost one in four young people reports that he or she is frequently depressed or has attempted suicide or has engaged in antisocial behavior (i.e., shoplifted, committed vandalism, or been in trouble with the police). As middle school ends, nearly 40 percent have engaged in a pattern of violent behavior, including hitting people, threatening to hurt people, or participating in a gang fight.

- The acceleration of those destructive middle school trends slows for high school youth, with the percentage who report engaging in antisocial behavior and violence and the percentage who report feeling depressed and suicidal stabilizing or declining through the rest of high school.

- However, reports of all of the other seven risk patterns increase throughout adolescence, with particularly large percentage jumps in reports of having had sexual intercourse, using tobacco, problem alcohol use, and using illicit drugs.

- Risk patterns that show a particularly large increase during the high school years are alcohol use, driving and alcohol, gambling, having sexual intercourse, and tobacco use. Between the 10th and 12th grades, each of those risk patterns increases by 25 percent or more. For example, the percentage having had sexual intercourse three or more times nearly doubles between grades 10 and 12. By the 12th grade, one-third or more of youth are engaging in each of these five high-risk patterns.

- Gender differences are quite dramatic on several of the high-risk patterns. Males are much more likely to report being engaged in antisocial behavior, gambling, problem alcohol use, school problems, and violence. Females are much more likely to report depression and/or suicide. Differences between males and females are minor on the other patterns.

- While the percentages are low for illicit drug use, sexual intercourse, and tobacco use in the 6th grade, it is troubling that any of these young people report having already developed these high-risk patterns.

- While school problems increase across time, the percentages reported here may be lower than reality because they do not reflect young people who have already dropped out of school.

Our hope is that youth become better able to *reduce* their risks as they get older. Ideally, they should become better decision makers, clearer about their own guiding values, and more convinced that they have options and supportive relationships. But just the reverse seems to happen: Most of the high-risk behavior patterns become more frequent among older youth. These data are not longitudinal (i.e., we did not follow the same youth for several years), so we cannot say that 6th graders will increasingly experience more risks as they develop into 12th graders. However, the fact that reports of most of the risks steadily increase from grade to grade strongly suggests that increased risky behavior is too common in adolescence.

FIGURE 3.4

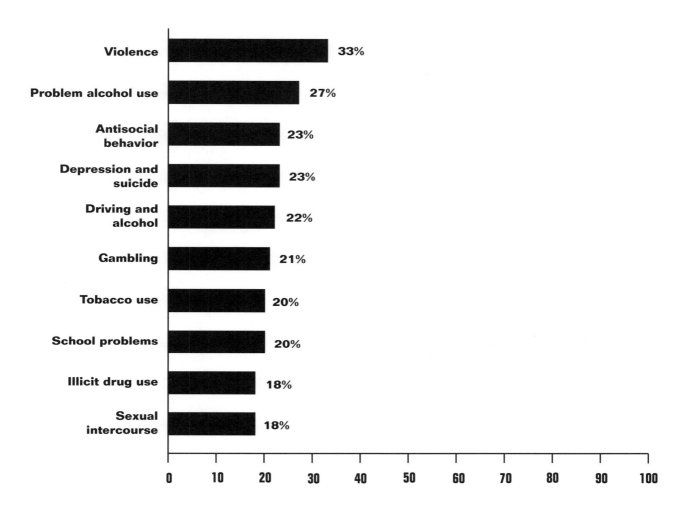

Youth Reporting Involvement in Patterns of High-Risk Behavior, in Descending Order of Prevalence

Violence — 33%
Problem alcohol use — 27%
Antisocial behavior — 23%
Depression and suicide — 23%
Driving and alcohol — 22%
Gambling — 21%
Tobacco use — 20%
School problems — 20%
Illicit drug use — 18%
Sexual intercourse — 18%

0 10 20 30 40 50 60 70 80 90 100

TABLE 3.6

Patterns of High-Risk Behavior, by Age and Gender (in %)

PATTERNS OF HIGH-RISK BEHAVIOR		ALL	GRADE						
			6	7	8	9	10	11	12
Problem alcohol use	All	27	11	14	23	28	33	38	41
	Females	23	8	11	20	25	30	32	35
	Males	31	13	17	25	31	37	44	48
Tobacco use	All	20	4	8	15	20	26	30	33
	Females	18	3	7	14	18	23	27	29
	Males	22	5	9	16	21	28	33	37
Illicit drug use	All	18	3	6	14	21	26	28	27
	Females	17	2	5	13	20	24	26	24
	Males	20	3	7	15	21	27	31	30
Sexual intercourse	All	18	3	6	9	14	23	34	45
	Females	19	2	3	7	13	24	37	49
	Males	18	4	8	11	14	21	30	42
Depression and suicide	All	23	19	20	24	25	25	24	22
	Females	29	20	24	31	33	34	31	28
	Males	16	17	16	18	16	16	17	16
Antisocial behavior	All	23	11	17	25	26	26	26	23
	Females	16	6	10	19	19	18	17	14
	Males	30	16	24	32	33	34	35	32
Violence	All	33	33	35	39	36	32	29	25
	Females	22	22	24	29	26	21	17	14
	Males	44	43	46	49	47	43	40	36
School problems	All	20	14	15	19	19	21	23	25
	Females	16	11	12	16	16	18	18	21
	Males	23	17	19	22	22	24	26	28
Driving and alcohol	All	22	12	14	19	21	25	30	34
	Females	21	10	13	17	20	25	28	30
	Males	23	13	15	21	22	25	32	37
Gambling	All	21	12	15	19	21	22	24	33
	Females	11	6	8	10	11	11	11	22
	Males	31	18	23	28	31	33	37	45

Engaging in Multiple High-Risk Behavior Patterns

One of the clear lessons learned from prevention efforts in the past two decades is that problems "travel together."[16] Young people who engage in one problem behavior often engage in others as well. Our data on high-risk behavior patterns support this understanding. One way we see this is by looking at the percentages of youth who report involvement in different numbers of high-risk behavior patterns (Figure 3.5 and Table 3.7).

Key findings

- One-third of young people report engaging in none of these high-risk behavior patterns. (Keep in mind, however, that many may still be experimenting with high-risk activity at levels below the threshold set for these high-risk patterns.)

- Two of every three young people report engaging in at least one high-risk pattern. Fully one in four youth engages in four or more of these patterns.

- In general, females report engaging in fewer high-risk behavior patterns than males. This dif-

ference is particularly marked among young people who report engaging in one of the patterns. Thirty-nine percent of females and 27 percent of males engage in none of the patterns.

- Older adolescents report more engagement in high-risk behavior patterns compared to younger adolescents. By 12th grade, 50 percent of youth report engaging in 3 or more of the 10 patterns.

These findings can be interpreted in several ways. First, it is encouraging that a sizable proportion of young people (33 percent) have not developed any of these high-risk patterns. While some of them are certainly experimenting with these problem behaviors, quality prevention and early intervention efforts can help to stop experimentation from becoming established, dangerous patterns. On the other hand, a sizable minority of young people have become trapped in highly destructive life patterns described by involvement in multiple risky patterns. Finding ways to reverse these patterns for this group of young people remains one of the pressing challenges facing our society.

---

[16] See, e.g., D. S. Elliott, "Health-Enhancing and Health-Compromising Lifestyles." In S. G. Millstein, A. C. Petersen, and E. O. Nightingale (eds.), *Promoting the Health of Adolescents: New Directions for the Twenty-first Century* (pp. 119-45). (New York: Oxford University Press, 1993); R. Jessor and S. L. Jessor, *Problem Behavior and Psychosocial Development: A Longitudinal Study of Youth* (New York: Academic, 1977).

FIGURE 3.5

Youth Who Report Engaging in Multiple High-Risk Behavior Patterns

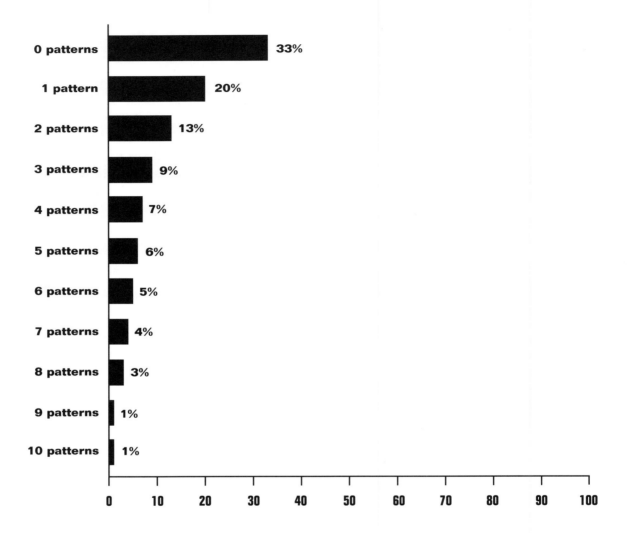

TABLE 3.7

Youth Who Report Engaging in Multiple High-Risk Behavior Patterns, by Grade and Gender (in %)

NUMBER OF HIGH-RISK BEHAVIOR PATTERNS		ALL	GRADE						
			6	7	8	9	10	11	12
0 patterns	**All**	**33**	**49**	**45**	**36**	**33**	**28**	**24**	**19**
	Females	39	57	53	43	38	33	29	22
	Males	27	40	37	29	27	23	19	15
1–2 patterns	**All**	**33**	**35**	**35**	**33**	**32**	**31**	**30**	**32**
	Females	32	32	32	31	32	32	32	34
	Males	33	39	37	34	33	31	29	29
3–4 patterns	**All**	**16**	**11**	**12**	**15**	**16**	**18**	**20**	**21**
	Females	14	7	8	13	14	16	19	21
	Males	18	14	15	18	19	19	21	21
5–6 patterns	**All**	**10**	**3**	**5**	**8**	**10**	**12**	**15**	**16**
	Females	9	2	4	7	9	11	13	15
	Males	12	5	7	10	11	13	16	18
7–10 patterns	**All**	**8**	**2**	**3**	**7**	**9**	**10**	**11**	**13**
	Females	6	1	2	6	7	8	8	8
	Males	10	3	4	8	10	12	15	17

High-Risk Behavior Patterns in Specific Subgroups of Youth

No group of young people is immune from the high-risk behavior patterns described in this chapter. At the same time, a notable percentage of youth in all groups make positive choices and do not engage in any of the high-risk behavior patterns.

However, there are important differences in levels of involvement by different groups. Figure 3.6 shows the number of high-risk behavior patterns in which the average surveyed young person in each subgroup engages. Table 3.8 shows the percentages of young people in each population who engage in different numbers of high-risk patterns. Although one-third of all youth experience no high-risk patterns, another third experience three or more patterns. In addition, Appendix C provides detailed statistics on each high-risk behavior pattern for each population.

It is important to note that looking only at "average" numbers of risk patterns hides the substantial proportions of even the most protected youth who report engaging in multiple risk behaviors. Even among the youth with the lowest average number of risk patterns—Asian American youth—fully one-quarter report experiencing three or more risk patterns, and nearly half or more of American Indian, Hispanic American, and multiracial youth experience three or more risk patterns.

Race/Ethnicity

Though we must exercise caution in generalizing this study's findings regarding race/ethnicity (because people of color are underrepresented in the sample, as are youth in major metropolitan areas), we do see some important differences among the youth surveyed.

Overall, American Indian youth tend to experience the greatest percentage of risk patterns, followed by multiracial and Hispanic American youth. Asian American

youth report the lowest levels of engagement, with White youth usually higher than but close to Asian American youth.

African American youth fall more in between, being relatively low on some risk patterns and high on others. For example, African American youth are the most likely to have engaged in sexual intercourse (31 percent), but, along with Asian American youth, the least likely to use tobacco every day (13 percent). The trends may be changing, however, as recent research shows that tobacco smoking has been on the rise among all youth, but especially among African American youth.[17]

The two risk patterns that appear to have the most striking differences among racial groups are school problems and violence. Only 16 to 18 percent of Asian American and White American youth have school problems (skipping school frequently and having below a C average), but 28 to 43 percent of American Indian, African American, Hispanic American, and multiracial youth have school problems. And, while the experience of violence is high even among Asian and White youth, it is still far lower than the percentages of American Indian, African American, Hispanic American, and multiracial youth who engage in violence.

Type of community

As in our analysis of deficits, American Indian youth who live on reservations experience much greater risks than other youth (about half the American Indian youth in our sample live on reservations). Indeed, only 10 percent of youth living on reservations are free of high-risk behavior patterns, compared to three times that many in other types of communities.

---

[17] Centers for Disease Control and Prevention, "Tobacco Use among High School Students—United States, 1997," *Morbidity and Mortality Weekly Report, 7,* no. 12 (April 3, 1998).

FIGURE 3.6

Average Number of 10 High-Risk Behavior Patterns Youth Report Being Engaged in, by Selected Variables

RACE/ETHNICITY

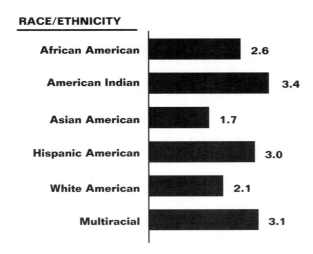

African American	2.6
American Indian	3.4
Asian American	1.7
Hispanic American	3.0
White American	2.1
Multiracial	3.1

TYPE OF COMMUNITY

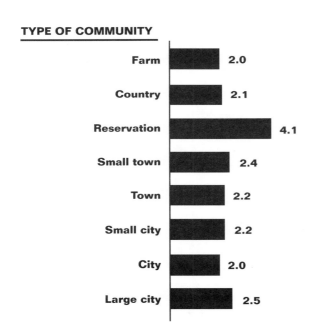

Farm	2.0
Country	2.1
Reservation	4.1
Small town	2.4
Town	2.2
Small city	2.2
City	2.0
Large city	2.5

MATERNAL EDUCATION

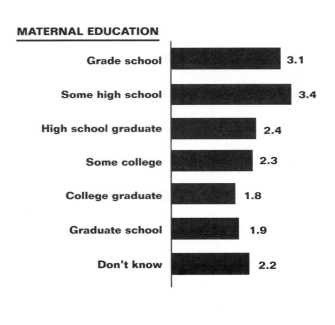

Grade school	3.1
Some high school	3.4
High school graduate	2.4
Some college	2.3
College graduate	1.8
Graduate school	1.9
Don't know	2.2

FAMILY COMPOSITION

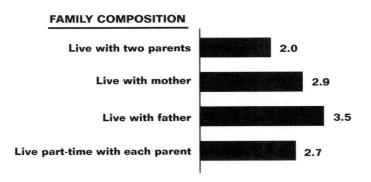

Live with two parents	2.0
Live with mother	2.9
Live with father	3.5
Live part-time with each parent	2.7

Youth who live on farms or in the country are generally, although not consistently, the least likely to experience these risk patterns. For example, farm youth do have the second-highest incidence of driving and alcohol use risks and an overall alcohol use percentage similar to that of all other youth surveyed except those living on reservations.

Except for the experience of violence, for which youth living on reservations (60 percent) and in large cities (40 percent) have the greatest risks, youth living in the largest metropolitan areas seem to have risk patterns comparable to those of most other youth (except youth living on farms, who generally have fewer risks). This finding probably understates the true experience of youth in large cities, since large cities are underrepresented in this sample and those that are included do not have disproportionate numbers of people living in distressed neighborhoods.

Maternal education

There is a similar, but even stronger, relationship between mother's education and high-risk behavior patterns than we saw between mother's education and youth deficits: For 8 of the 10 risk patterns, youth whose mothers had only some high school are more likely to engage in these patterns than youth whose mothers had even less education (grade school only) or more education (high school graduate or beyond). The only exceptions are that youth whose mothers had only a grade school education are the most likely to experience school problems and violence; those two risk patterns generally decline with each increase in mother's education.

Family composition

Youth from two-parent families consistently report the lowest levels of involvement in high-risk behavior patterns in comparison to other types of families. Two-parent families seem especially to offer protection against school problems, use of illicit drugs, sexual intercourse, tobacco use, antisocial behavior, and depression and suicide. For example, only 17 percent of youth in two-parent families experience school problems, while 24 percent of students do who live part-

time with both parents, 30 percent if they live only with mother, and 34 percent—twice the proportion of youth from two-parent homes—if they live only with their father.

Youth who live only with their fathers consistently report the greatest experience of risk patterns. Joint custody arrangements may offer some protection in that youth who live part-time with each parent report lower levels of involvement in five of the patterns than those who live with just their father or just their mother. For the other five risk patterns, the levels of involvement are similar to the levels of those living only with their mother (which are lower than the levels of those living only with their father).

Summary

As was the case for deficits, youth living in two-parent families and those whose mothers have more education (in the case of risk patterns, at least a high school diploma) are much less likely to engage in these high-risk behavior patterns. Stable parental relationships and high parental education clearly offer substantial protection from risk.

Youth who appear more likely to engage in the high-risk patterns are those whose mothers completed only some high school, students not living in two-parent families, and American Indian, multiracial, and Hispanic American youth. Youth who appear least likely to engage in the risk patterns are those living on farms, those whose mothers graduated from college, youth living in two-parent families, and Asian American youth.

It is important to examine these differences to determine factors that lead to these variations in subpopulations of youth and then to take action to address injustices and systemic issues that perpetuate the problems. It is just as important to recognize that no circumstances make young people entirely immune from these high-risk patterns and no circumstances make problems inevitable; many young people from the groups studied do avoid getting involved in most of these problem behavior patterns. Thus, there is much strength and resiliency to build on as we seek to address these concerns.

TABLE 3.8

Youth Who Report Engagement in Multiple High-Risk Behavior Patterns, by Selected Variables

	Average Number of High-Risk Behavior Patterns	PERCENTAGE ENGAGING IN EACH NUMBER OF HIGH-RISK BEHAVIOR PATTERNS				
		0 Patterns	1–2 Patterns	3–4 Patterns	5–6 Patterns	7–10 Patterns
All	2.2	33	33	16	10	8
Race/Ethnicity						
African American	2.6	22	37	20	10	11
American Indian	3.4	16	29	20	17	18
Asian American	1.7	39	36	13	7	6
Hispanic American	3.0	20	31	21	15	13
White American	2.1	35	33	16	10	7
Multiracial	3.1	21	31	19	14	15
Type of Community						
Farm	2.0	34	34	16	9	6
Country	2.1	33	33	16	10	8
Reservation	4.1	10	26	21	20	23
Small town	2.4	30	33	17	11	9
Town	2.2	33	32	16	11	8
Small city	2.2	34	32	16	10	8
City	2.0	37	32	15	9	7
Large city	2.5	29	31	17	11	12
Maternal Education						
Grade school	3.1	19	33	20	13	16
Some high school	3.4	17	29	21	16	17
High school graduate	2.4	29	33	18	12	9
Some college	2.3	31	33	17	11	8
College graduate	1.8	39	32	14	8	6
Graduate school	1.9	40	32	14	8	7
Don't know	2.2	31	36	16	9	8
Family Composition						
Live with two parents	2.0	36	33	15	9	7
Live with mother	2.9	22	31	20	14	13
Live with father	3.5	15	29	21	17	17
Live part-time with each parent	2.7	26	33	18	12	12

The Clustering of High-Risk Behavior Patterns ——

In the past two decades, social scientists have demonstrated that risks tend to cluster. So, for example, a young person who frequently uses tobacco is more likely to engage in sexual intercourse than a young person not already using tobacco. As shown in Table 3.9, our data consistently confirm this clustering, or co-occurrence, of risks, sometimes in dramatic fashion. Young people who are already engaged in one high-risk behavior pattern are much more likely to engage in another pattern.

For example, 71 percent of young people who regularly use tobacco also regularly use alcohol. In contrast, only 17 percent of young people who abstain from tobacco use report alcohol use. Similarly, the well-known relationship between alcohol use and sexual intercourse is evident in these data. Forty percent of youth who engage in problem alcohol use have also had sexual intercourse three or more times, compared with just 10 percent of youth who do not engage in problem alcohol use.

Overall, the risky behavior patterns that seem most likely to co-occur with experiencing other risky behavior patterns are the substance use patterns (problem alcohol use, illicit drug use, and tobacco use, and, to a lesser extent, driving and alcohol). Youth who engage in substance use are more likely than other youth to engage in other risk patterns.

TABLE 3.9

Co-Occurrence of Risk Patterns: Youth Likely to Report Engaging in Additional Behavior Patterns with Engagement in One Pattern (in %)

	PROBLEM ALCOHOL USE	TOBACCO USE	ILLICIT DRUG USE	SEXUAL INTER-COURSE	DEPRESSION AND SUICIDE	ANTISOCIAL BEHAVIOR	VIOLENCE	SCHOOL PROBLEMS	DRIVING AND ALCOHOL	GAMBLING
Problem alcohol use										
If engaged in, then	–	51	48	40	34	49	56	39	50	37
If not engaged in, then	–	8	7	10	19	13	25	12	11	15
Tobacco use										
If engaged in, then	71	–	59	49	39	54	59	46	51	36
If not engaged in, then	17	–	8	11	19	15	27	13	15	17
Illicit drug use										
If engaged in, then	71	63	–	50	40	59	60	45	53	38
If not engaged in, then	17	10	–	11	19	14	27	13	15	17
Sexual intercourse										
If engaged in, then	59	52	50	–	38	45	52	40	47	35
If not engaged in, then	20	12	11	–	20	18	29	15	16	18
Depression and suicide										
If engaged in, then	40	34	32	30	–	36	50	32	32	23
If not engaged in, then	23	15	14	15	–	19	28	16	19	20
Antisocial behavior										
If engaged in, then	58	47	48	36	36	–	69	43	44	40
If not engaged in, then	18	12	10	13	19	–	22	13	15	15
Violence										
If engaged in, then	45	35	34	29	34	48	–	34	36	37
If not engaged in, then	18	12	11	13	17	10	–	12	15	13
School problems										
If engaged in, then	55	46	43	38	38	50	58	–	42	32
If not engaged in, then	20	13	12	14	19	16	27	–	17	18
Driving and alcohol										
If engaged in, then	62	45	44	40	34	46	55	37	–	37
If not engaged in, then	17	12	11	12	20	16	27	15	–	16
Gambling										
If engaged in, then	48	34	33	31	26	44	59	30	39	–
If not engaged in, then	22	16	14	15	22	17	26	16	17	–

Differences between Middle and High School Youth

Table 3.10 illustrates the differential negative influences for middle school and high school youth that engaging in one risk pattern has on their chances of engaging in others.

Four high-risk behavior patterns are especially detrimental to middle school youth in that they greatly increase the likelihood that young adolescents will engage in other high-risk patterns: problem alcohol use, illicit drug use, tobacco use, and sexual intercourse. For high school youth, engaging in violence particularly increases the likelihood that the older youth will engage in all the other risk patterns as well.

For both middle and high school youth, those who report engaging in those respective high-risk behavior patterns are different from the typical youth in that age-group. That developmental difference—being "out of sync" with their peers—connects them to a constellation of other less responsible youth and other risky behaviors. For example, high school youth report experiencing decreasing involvement in violence compared to middle school youth. Some youth, however, maintain or increase their involvement in violent behavior, which isolates them from most of their peers, thereby increasing their susceptibility to additional risks.

Thus, we see reflected in these data what we read about in newspaper accounts of young people who commit violent crimes: That a small percentage of young people become increasingly distinct from their peers. This difference often isolates them from the majority of their peers, places them in contact with more negative influences, and increases the probability that their behavior will become more and more dangerous and destructive.

TABLE 3.10

Co-Occurrence of Risk Patterns among Middle and High School Youth (%)

GRADE	PROBLEM ALCOHOL USE		TOBACCO USE		ILLICIT DRUG USE		SEXUAL INTER-COURSE		DEPRESSION AND SUICIDE		ANTISOCIAL BEHAVIOR		VIOLENCE		SCHOOL PROBLEMS		DRIVING AND ALCOHOL		GAMBLING	
	6–8	9–12	6–8	9–12	6–8	9–12	6–8	9–12	6–8	9–12	6–8	9–12	6–8	9–12	6–8	9–12	6–8	9–12	6–8	9–12
Problem alcohol use	–	–	40	54	36	52	23	46	42	31	57	46	72	50	41	39	40	54	36	37
Tobacco use	69	71	–	–	52	61	31	53	50	37	69	51	79	54	51	45	45	52	36	36
Illicit drug use	71	71	59	64	–	–	36	53	51	37	74	56	81	56	51	44	49	53	41	37
Sexual intercourse	61	59	47	53	48	50	–	–	49	36	65	42	81	47	48	39	46	47	41	34
Depression and suicide	33	44	23	40	20	39	14	40	–	–	37	36	58	45	31	33	27	35	23	24
Antisocial behavior	50	62	35	52	33	55	22	44	41	34	–	–	80	64	41	43	36	48	37	41
Violence	33	55	21	45	19	45	14	40	34	34	41	52	–	–	29	38	28	43	32	41
School problems	41	62	30	55	26	52	18	48	40	37	48	51	64	55	–	–	31	47	27	35
Driving and alcohol	43	69	29	52	28	51	19	47	38	32	45	46	67	51	34	38	–	–	35	38
Gambling	37	53	21	39	21	38	16	38	30	24	44	43	71	53	27	31	34	41	–	–

Does One Risk Lead to Another?

Sometimes we talk about some behaviors being "gateways" to others, behaviors that increase the chances that young people will get involved in many different problems (e.g., marijuana use as a gateway to more serious drug use). Though our survey data cannot show an actual cause-effect relationship, they do suggest definite patterns that support such a perspective.

As shown in Figure 3.7, having any one of the high-risk patterns not only increases the chance that youth will also engage in a second risk pattern, it dramatically raises the probability they will engage in three or more of the 10 high-risk behavior patterns. Young people involved in any one of the risk patterns are several times more likely to engage in three or more risk patterns than youth who avoid these patterns.

This relation is particularly borne out in high-risk behaviors such as problem alcohol use, illicit drug use, tobacco use, and antisocial behavior. If a student engages in any one of those risk patterns, he or she is more than four times as likely as other students to engage in three or more high-risk behavior patterns.

FIGURE 3.7

Youth Reporting Three or More Risk Patterns, If Already Reporting One

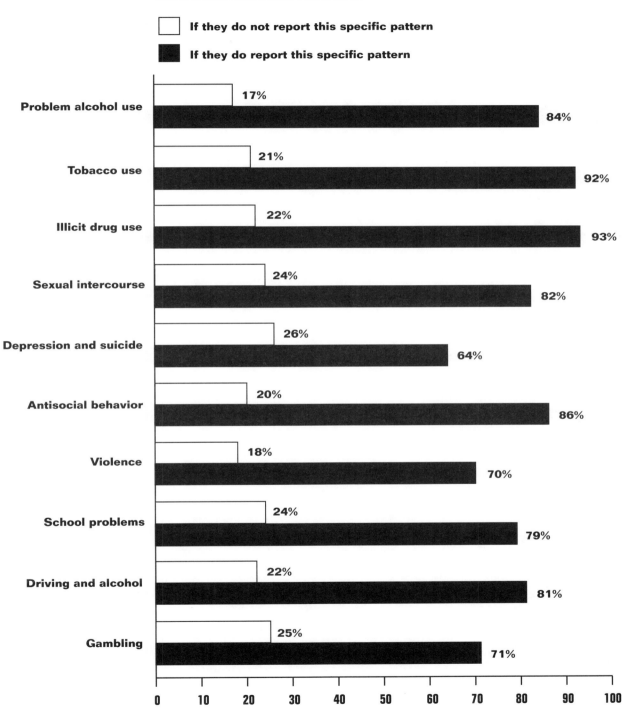

PERCENTAGE WHO REPORT THREE OR MORE
HIGH-RISK BEHAVIOR PATTERNS

☐ If they do not report this specific pattern

■ If they do report this specific pattern

Problem alcohol use — 17% / 84%

Tobacco use — 21% / 92%

Illicit drug use — 22% / 93%

Sexual intercourse — 24% / 82%

Depression and suicide — 26% / 64%

Antisocial behavior — 20% / 86%

Violence — 18% / 70%

School problems — 24% / 79%

Driving and alcohol — 22% / 81%

Gambling — 25% / 71%

0 10 20 30 40 50 60 70 80 90 100

Overcoming Immobilization

One of the dangers in presenting in-depth information on young people's deficits and involvement in high-risk behaviors is that it can lead readers to despair and a sense of powerlessness, rather than inspiring them to get involved and take action to make a difference. After all, we have learned in recent decades how complex many of these issues are, and we know how difficult it can be to break cycles of abuse, chemical use, violence, depression, and other problems addressed in this chapter.

This reaction to problems young people face was captured in a Public Agenda study of why adults do and do not get involved in children's issues: "The public's definition of the problem—which focuses on broad moral and economic problems—makes them feel that there is very little that can be done to help children. Their tolerance for the problems of children stems, in other words, not from indifference but from a feeling of helplessness."[18]

As we work to strengthen young people's developmental foundation and increase the odds that they will grow up healthy, we also need to find ways to mobilize every person—parent, neighbor, youth worker, teacher, friend—to do what he or she can to reduce these problems in young people's lives.

The developmental assets offer a hopeful strategy for reaching this goal, since building assets is a positive thing that everyone can do for youth. As we will see in the next chapter, the developmental assets have a powerful impact in young people's lives, reducing the likelihood that young people will engage in risky behaviors and counterbalancing the negative impact of developmental deficits. In short, they provide key building blocks in a solid foundation for life.

[18] John Immerwahr, *Talking about Children: A Focus Group Report from Public Agenda* (New York: Public Agenda, 1995), 1.

The Power of Developmental Assets

4

In the previous two chapters, we have looked at young people's experiences of developmental assets (Chapter 2) and their experiences of deficits and high-risk behaviors (Chapter 3). This chapter draws these pieces together, showing the connections between developmental assets and young people's behaviors, both positive and negative.

As we will see, developmental assets are powerful predictors of behavior. They appear to play three critical roles in young people's lives:

1. They serve as **protective factors,** helping to "inoculate" youth against many forms of high-risk behavior, including alcohol and other drug use, violence, school failure, sexual intercourse, and the other high-risk behavior patterns identified in Chapter 3.

2. The 40 assets serve as **enhancement factors.** By this we mean they help to increase the probability that youth will engage in thriving behaviors such as helping others, leadership, and being intentional about nutrition and exercise.

3. They help youth weather adversity. In this way, developmental assets are **resiliency factors,** assisting young people to minimize the destructive consequences of threats to their development, including the deficits presented in Chapter 3.

Perhaps the core message of asset building lies in this chapter: That is, the greater the number of assets, the better the outcomes for all young people, including those who are vulnerable as a result of other threats and challenges in their lives. As assets increase in number, many forms of high-risk behavior decrease. As assets increase in number, many forms of thriving increase.

While this report establishes a strong relation or correlation between assets and behavioral outcomes, the data in this report do not establish a cause-effect relationship. That conclusion would need to be tested in studies using other research designs. However, a comprehensive review of the scientific literature provides compelling evidence that many of the assets have a direct impact on behavior.[1] Additional information about the power of the assets can be found in several recent scientific publications, which are listed at the end of Chapter 1.

---

[1] Peter C. Scales and Nancy Leffert, *Developmental Assets: A Synthesis of the Scientific Research on Adolescent Development* (Minneapolis: Search Institute, 1999).

The Protective Power
of Developmental Assets

In Chapter 3, we defined and discussed 10 patterns of high-risk behavior: antisocial behavior; depression and/or suicide; driving and alcohol; gambling; illicit drug use; problem alcohol use; school problems; sexual intercourse; tobacco use; and violence. How do the assets impact each of these 10 patterns of high-risk behavior?

One way to understand the relationship between assets and the patterns of risky behavior is to group young people into four categories based on the number of assets they have:

- Youth with 0 to 10 assets;

- Youth with 11 to 20 assets;

- Youth with 21 to 30 assets; and

- Youth with 31 to 40 assets.

These four categories represent arbitrary (though reasonable) markers of levels of assets, based on quartiles, ranging from low-asset youth (0-10 assets) to asset-rich youth (31-40 assets). As shown in Figures 4.1 through 4.10 and Tables 4.1 through 4.10, the more assets young people have, the less likely they are to engage in each of the 10 patterns of high-risk behavior.

Figure 4.1, for example, focuses on problem alcohol use. Of those youth who have 0 to 10 assets, 53 percent report problem alcohol use (using alcohol three or more times in the last month or being intoxicated once or more in the past two weeks). For youth with 11 to 20 assets, the percentage falls to 30. For those with 21 to 30 assets, the percentage tumbles to 11.

And finally, among youth with a high number of assets (31-40), only 3 percent engage in problem alcohol use.

Figures 4.2 through 4.10 show essentially the same relationship for each of the other high-risk behavior patterns. Thus, across many different forms of health-compromising behaviors, rates for such behavior are dramatically reduced as the number of assets increases. Furthermore, as shown in Tables 4.1 through 4.10, this connection between assets and risk behaviors is strong for all ages of youth and for both females and males.

We have observed this important connection between assets and risk behavior across hundreds of communities studied. And, as shown in the Appendixes, these same types of patterns are repeated for different subgroups of youth:

- Each of the racial/ethnic groups of youth represented in this study;

- Youth from all types of families;

- Youth in different types of communities; and

- Youth whose mothers have different levels of education (an approximate measure of family income).

The point here is that the assets are cumulative: the more the better. And they have a wide-ranging influence, impacting many forms of behavior that can compromise young people's personal health and well-being.

FIGURE 4.1

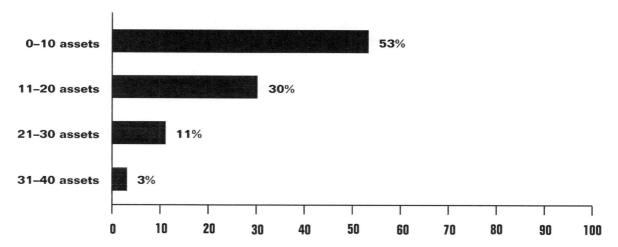

Protective Consequences of Developmental Assets: Problem Alcohol Use

Percentage of youth reporting they have used alcohol three or more times in the past 30 days or have gotten drunk once or more in the past two weeks.

0–10 assets   53%

11–20 assets   30%

21–30 assets   11%

31–40 assets   3%

0   10   20   30   40   50   60   70   80   90   100

TABLE 4.1

Problem Alcohol Use, by Level of Assets, by Grade and Gender (in %)

LEVEL OF ASSETS		ALL	GRADE						
			6	7	8	9	10	11	12
0–10 assets	All	53	31	39	46	55	58	61	66
	Females	52	31	39	47	55	58	57	62
	Males	54	30	39	46	54	58	62	67
11–20 assets	All	30	14	16	24	29	35	41	45
	Females	29	12	15	24	29	34	37	40
	Males	31	15	17	24	29	32	44	49
21–30 assets	All	11	5	5	8	11	14	19	22
	Females	11	4	4	7	11	13	16	21
	Males	13	6	6	10	11	15	23	23
31–40 assets	All	3	2	1	2	2	5	5	10
	Females	3	2	1	1	2	6	6	10
	Males	3	3	1	3	3	4	5	10

FIGURE 4.2

Protective Consequences of Developmental Assets: Tobacco Use

Percentage of youth reporting they smoke one or more cigarettes every day or use chewing tobacco frequently.

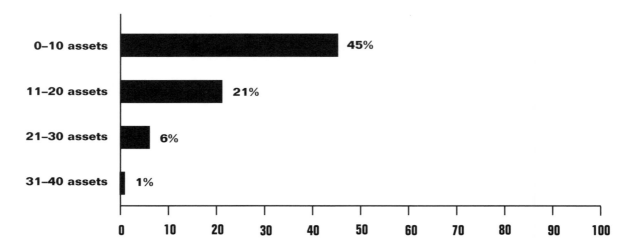

TABLE 4.2

Tobacco Use, by Level of Assets, by Grade and Gender (in %)

LEVEL OF ASSETS		ALL	GRADE						
			6	7	8	9	10	11	12
0–10 assets	All	45	17	25	37	45	52	55	58
	Females	48	20	28	40	50	55	57	60
	Males	43	15	24	36	42	51	55	57
11–20 assets	All	21	5	8	14	18	25	32	35
	Females	21	5	8	14	20	25	32	34
	Males	20	5	8	14	17	25	31	36
21–30 assets	All	6	1	2	3	5	8	11	14
	Females	6	1	2	3	4	8	10	14
	Males	6	2	2	4	6	8	13	15
31–40 assets	All	1	0	0	1	1	2	3	5
	Females	1	0	0	1	1	2	3	4
	Males	1	0	0	1	1	2	3	8

FIGURE 4.3

Protective Consequences of Developmental Assets: Illicit Drug Use

Percentage of youth reporting they have used illicit drugs three or more times in the past 12 months.

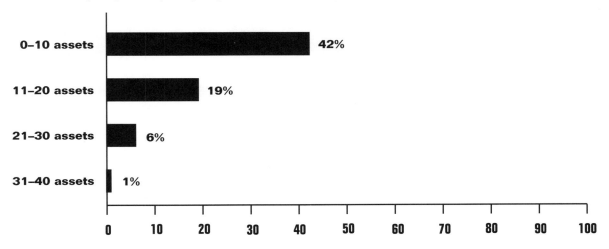

TABLE 4.3

Illicit Drug Use, by Level of Assets, by Grade and Gender (in %)

LEVEL OF ASSETS		ALL	GRADE						
			6	7	8	9	10	11	12
0–10 assets	All	42	12	22	36	46	50	51	49
	Females	45	14	25	38	51	53	54	51
	Males	40	11	21	34	43	48	49	47
11–20 assets	All	19	3	6	13	20	26	30	28
	Females	20	3	5	14	22	27	30	27
	Males	19	3	6	12	18	24	27	29
21–30 assets	All	6	1	1	3	6	8	11	12
	Females	6	1	1	3	6	8	10	12
	Males	6	1	1	3	7	8	13	11
31–40 assets	All	1	0	0	0	1	1	3	3
	Females	1	0	0	1	1	1	3	3
	Males	1	1	0	0	1	2	4	5

FIGURE 4.4

Protective Consequences of Developmental Assets: Sexual Intercourse

Percentage of youth reporting they have had sexual intercourse three or more times in their lifetime.

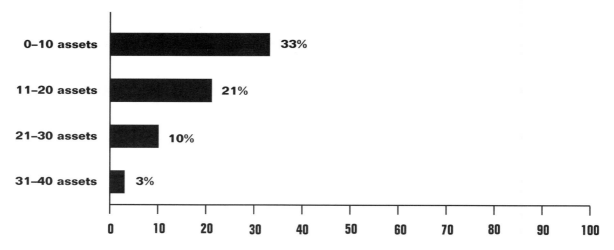

TABLE 4.4

Sexual Intercourse, by Level of Assets, by Grade and Gender (in %)

LEVEL OF ASSETS		ALL	GRADE						
			6	7	8	9	10	11	12
0–10 assets	All	33	8	16	20	28	38	47	59
	Females	36	7	14	19	30	46	58	69
	Males	30	9	17	20	26	34	41	54
11–20 assets	All	21	4	6	9	13	23	36	49
	Females	23	2	4	8	14	27	43	55
	Males	18	5	7	10	12	18	29	43
21–30 assets	All	10	1	2	3	5	11	21	34
	Females	11	0	1	2	5	13	24	38
	Males	8	2	4	4	5	8	17	26
31–40 assets	All	3	1	1	1	2	4	10	17
	Females	3	0	0	1	2	5	11	16
	Males	3	2	1	1	2	4	8	19

FIGURE 4.5

Protective Consequences of Developmental Assets: Depression and/or Attempted Suicide

Percentage of youth reporting that they are frequently depressed and/or have attempted suicide.

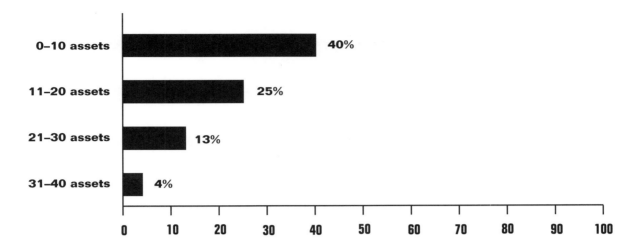

TABLE 4.5

Depression and/or Attempted Suicide, by Level of Assets, by Grade and Gender (in %)

LEVEL OF ASSETS		ALL	GRADE						
			6	7	8	9	10	11	12
0–10 assets	All	40	45	42	44	42	39	38	34
	Females	58	59	57	61	63	57	55	51
	Males	29	38	33	32	29	27	27	26
11–20 assets	All	25	26	23	26	26	27	25	23
	Females	36	32	34	37	38	39	35	32
	Males	15	21	14	16	14	14	16	14
21–30 assets	All	13	12	12	12	13	13	14	13
	Females	16	14	14	16	18	18	18	17
	Males	7	9	8	7	6	6	8	8
31–40 assets	All	4	4	4	4	5	5	5	4
	Females	5	4	4	5	6	7	5	5
	Males	3	5	4	2	3	1	3	2

FIGURE 4.6

Protective Consequences of Developmental Assets: Antisocial Behavior

Percentage of youth reporting they have been involved in three or more incidents of shoplifting, trouble with police, or vandalism in the past 12 months.

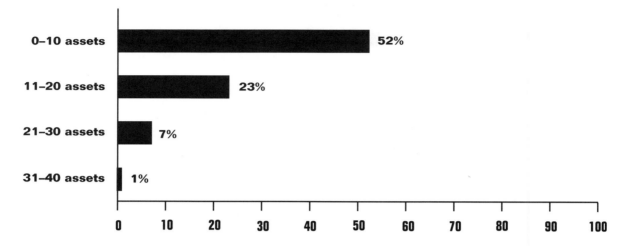

TABLE 4.6

Antisocial Behavior, by Level of Assets, by Grade and Gender (in %)

LEVEL OF ASSETS		ALL	GRADE						
			6	7	8	9	10	11	12
0–10 assets	All	52	39	48	56	55	54	51	47
	Females	45	36	39	52	49	47	40	36
	Males	56	40	53	59	60	58	57	52
11–20 assets	All	23	15	18	25	26	25	26	23
	Females	18	8	13	21	21	18	18	15
	Males	29	19	23	30	30	31	34	30
21–30 assets	All	7	4	6	8	8	8	8	8
	Females	5	2	3	6	6	5	5	5
	Males	11	7	9	12	10	12	13	14
31–40 assets	All	1	1	1	2	2	2	2	2
	Females	1	0	0	1	1	1	2	1
	Males	3	2	1	5	3	4	3	5

FIGURE 4.7

Protective Consequences of Developmental Assets: Violence

Percentage of youth reporting they have engaged in three or more acts of fighting, hitting, injuring a person, carrying or using a weapon, or threatening physical harm in the past 12 months.

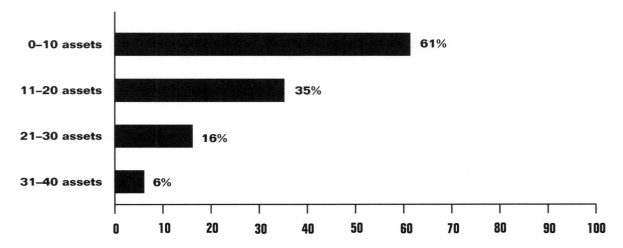

TABLE 4.7

Violence, by Level of Assets, by Grade and Gender (in %)

LEVEL OF ASSETS		ALL	GRADE						
			6	7	8	9	10	11	12
0–10 assets	All	61	70	70	68	65	58	52	49
	Females	51	60	61	60	55	47	40	38
	Males	67	75	76	73	72	64	59	54
11–20 assets	All	35	44	42	43	38	32	29	25
	Females	26	33	32	34	29	22	19	15
	Males	45	52	50	50	46	41	39	35
21–30 assets	All	16	22	21	19	16	13	12	11
	Females	11	16	14	13	11	8	6	7
	Males	25	29	29	28	25	21	20	18
31–40 assets	All	6	9	8	7	6	4	3	2
	Females	4	6	5	5	3	2	1	1
	Males	11	15	14	12	10	8	4	6

FIGURE 4.8

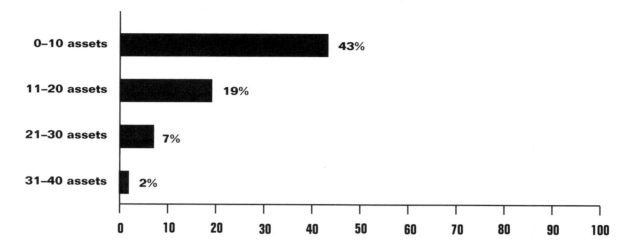

Protective Consequences of Developmental Assets: School Problems

Percentage of youth reporting they have skipped school two or more days in the past four weeks and/or have below a C average.

TABLE 4.8

School Problems, by Level of Assets, by Grade and Gender (in %)

LEVEL OF ASSETS		ALL	GRADE						
			6	7	8	9	10	11	12
0–10 assets	**All**	**43**	**32**	**39**	**42**	**43**	**45**	**45**	**49**
	Females	41	30	36	39	41	45	42	49
	Males	44	34	40	44	44	45	47	49
11–20 assets	**All**	**19**	**18**	**16**	**18**	**17**	**18**	**21**	**24**
	Females	18	15	15	17	16	18	20	23
	Males	20	19	17	19	18	19	22	25
21–30 assets	**All**	**7**	**8**	**7**	**7**	**6**	**6**	**8**	**10**
	Females	6	7	6	6	5	6	7	10
	Males	8	10	8	7	7	7	10	10
31–40 assets	**All**	**2**	**3**	**2**	**2**	**2**	**2**	**2**	**5**
	Females	2	2	2	1	2	2	2	4
	Males	4	4	3	4	3	2	3	7

FIGURE 4.9

Protective Consequences of Developmental Assets: Driving and Alcohol

Percentage of youth reporting they have driven after drinking or ridden with a drinking driver three or more times in the past 12 months.

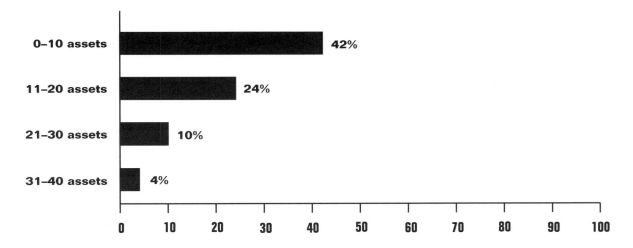

TABLE 4.9

Driving and Alcohol, by Level of Assets, by Grade and Gender (in %)

LEVEL OF ASSETS		ALL	GRADE						
			6	7	8	9	10	11	12
0–10 assets	**All**	**42**	**26**	**31**	**36**	**39**	**44**	**50**	**57**
	Females	42	28	33	36	40	47	49	57
	Males	41	25	30	37	38	42	51	56
11–20 assets	**All**	**24**	**15**	**16**	**20**	**21**	**27**	**32**	**35**
	Females	26	15	17	20	23	29	33	35
	Males	23	15	15	19	19	24	30	36
21–30 assets	**All**	**10**	**7**	**7**	**9**	**9**	**11**	**15**	**17**
	Females	11	7	7	8	10	12	15	18
	Males	10	7	7	10	9	9	14	16
31–40 assets	**All**	**4**	**4**	**3**	**3**	**4**	**6**	**4**	**8**
	Females	4	4	3	2	3	6	4	9
	Males	4	4	4	3	5	4	3	7

FIGURE 4.10

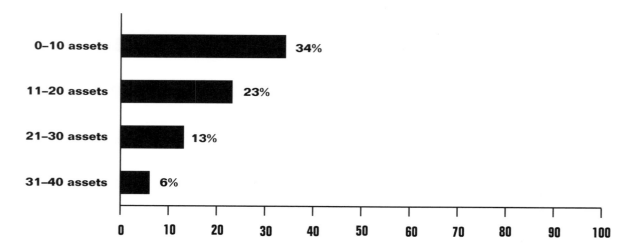

Protective Consequences of Developmental Assets: Gambling

Percentage of youth reporting they have gambled three or more times in the past 12 months.

TABLE 4.10

Gambling, by Level of Assets, by Grade and Gender (in %)

LEVEL OF ASSETS		ALL	GRADE						
			6	7	8	9	10	11	12
0–10 assets	**All**	**34**	**28**	**31**	**31**	**33**	**33**	**34**	**47**
	Females	20	19	18	19	18	19	17	34
	Males	42	32	38	39	42	42	44	54
11–20 assets	**All**	**23**	**16**	**17**	**21**	**22**	**23**	**25**	**36**
	Females	13	9	10	12	12	12	13	24
	Males	32	21	24	29	32	34	37	47
21–30 assets	**All**	**13**	**8**	**10**	**11**	**12**	**13**	**15**	**23**
	Females	7	4	5	6	7	7	7	16
	Males	21	12	15	18	21	23	28	35
31–40 assets	**All**	**6**	**3**	**4**	**6**	**5**	**7**	**7**	**15**
	Females	3	1	2	3	3	3	4	11
	Males	12	7	9	14	9	16	15	27

Impact on Multiple High-Risk Behavior Patterns

The previous pages show the connections between levels of assets and each of the 10 patterns of high-risk behavior. As shown in Figure 4.11, the average number of high-risk behavior patterns young people report engaging in also changes dramatically based on the number of assets in their lives. Youth with high levels of assets (31-40) engage, on average, in just 0.3 of the 10 patterns of high-risk behavior. In contrast, on average, youth with few assets (0-10) report engaging in 4.4 of these 10 patterns.

Thus, while having most of the 40 assets does not eliminate all problem behaviors (some youth with many assets still engage in some high-risk behaviors), it does dramatically reduce the proportion of young people engaging in each high-risk behavior pattern, as well as the proportion of youth who are engaging in multiple risky behavior patterns.

FIGURE 4.11

Average Number of 10 High-Risk Behavior Patterns, by Level of Assets

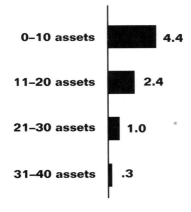

0–10 assets 4.4

11–20 assets 2.4

21–30 assets 1.0

31–40 assets .3

The Enhancement Power of Developmental Assets

Healthy development for American youth should not be defined only as the avoidance of risky behavior. We ought also to conceptualize and assess the positive attitudes and behaviors we seek to promote. These markers of developmental success might include school success, valuing diversity, leadership skills, and work skills, as well as a host of others.

To approximate a definition of thriving, our studies explore eight behaviors, skills, and dispositions that we think are essential for successful development (see Table 4.11). We do not suggest that these are the only eight elements of thriving, but they are a starting point. (See Appendix D for the items used to measure thriving behaviors, as well as detailed findings on thriving behaviors among selected groups of youth.)

Key findings

- The thriving behaviors of school success, helping others, and overcoming adversity are relatively stable across grades 6 to 12. School success is experienced by only one-quarter of youth, while the other two thriving behaviors are common among the great majority.

- Reports of leadership go up across grades 6 to 12, and this asset is experienced by about 70 percent of youth.

- Reports of valuing diversity, maintaining health, resisting danger, and delaying gratification all go down across middle and high school, with a particularly large drop in the middle grades on resisting danger.

- The majority of 6th graders report experiencing six of the eight thriving behaviors (only school success and resisting danger are experienced by just a minority of 6th graders). But by the 12th grade, only a minority report maintaining good health habits or delaying gratification, and only a bare majority—51 percent—report valuing diversity.

- Reports from males especially decrease in valuing diversity and resisting danger.

- Reports from females especially decrease in maintaining health. Females in middle school report greater healthy habits, but by the 9th grade, males begin reporting better health habits than females.

- Males report more delay of gratification and ability to overcome adversity.

Figure 4.12 and Table 4.12 show that some of these thriving indicators (e.g., exhibits leadership and overcomes adversity, reported by 68 percent and 71 percent of our sample, respectively) are experienced by most of the young people surveyed. Other thriving indicators (e.g., succeeds in school and resists danger, reported by only 23 percent and 20 percent, respectively) are experienced by relatively small proportions of young people.

Figures 4.13 to 4.20 display the percentages of youth reporting each of these indicators, as a function of how many assets they have (0-10, 11-20, 21-30, 31-40). As was the case with risk behaviors, we see a strong theme about the power of the assets. For each of the eight indicators, the percentages increase as the level of assets increases. For example, reports of school success rise from 7 percent of youth with 0 to 10 assets to 53 percent for those with 31 to 40 assets. The same patterns are evident for all subgroups of youth, as shown in Tables 4.13 to 4.20 and the Appendixes.

These findings add strength to the idea that the assets are cumulative (the more the better) and comprehensive (i.e., they inform many behavioral outcomes).

TABLE 4.11

Definitions of Thriving Indicators

THRIVING INDICATOR	DEFINITION
Succeeds in school	Gets mostly A's on report card.
Helps others	Helps friends or neighbors one or more hours per week.
Values diversity	Places high importance on getting to know people of other racial/ethnic groups.
Maintains good health	Pays attention to healthy nutrition and exercise.
Exhibits leadership	Has been a leader of a group or organization in the past 12 months.
Resists danger	Avoids doing things that are dangerous.
Delays gratification	Saves money for something special rather than spending it all right away.
Overcomes adversity	Does not give up when things get difficult.

FIGURE 4.12

Youth Who Report Experiencing Thriving Indicators, in Descending Order

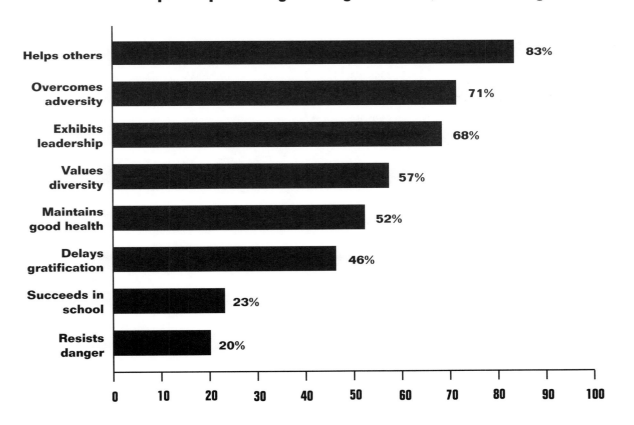

TABLE 4.12

Thriving Indicators, by Grade and Gender (in %)

THRIVING INDICATOR		ALL	GRADE						
			6	7	8	9	10	11	12
Succeeds in school	All	23	24	26	25	23	21	21	23
	Females	28	29	32	30	26	26	26	29
	Males	19	20	21	20	19	16	16	18
Helps others	All	83	86	84	83	83	83	83	83
	Females	88	90	89	87	88	87	87	86
	Males	79	83	80	78	78	78	80	80
Values diversity	All	57	64	62	58	56	53	51	51
	Females	67	70	69	68	67	66	63	63
	Males	46	59	54	48	45	41	40	40
Maintains good health	All	52	61	58	54	51	48	47	45
	Females	52	64	60	55	50	47	45	43
	Males	52	58	56	53	53	49	48	47
Exhibits leadership	All	68	65	65	67	67	67	70	74
	Females	69	66	65	67	68	70	72	75
	Males	67	64	65	66	66	65	68	73
Resists danger	All	20	29	24	18	17	16	17	19
	Females	26	37	31	23	22	22	24	26
	Males	13	21	17	13	12	10	11	11
Delays gratification	All	46	52	50	46	44	43	43	43
	Females	44	51	49	43	41	40	43	44
	Males	47	53	50	49	48	45	44	43
Overcomes adversity	All	71	70	69	69	71	71	72	75
	Females	69	69	69	67	68	68	70	72
	Males	73	70	70	71	73	73	74	77

FIGURE 4.13 —————————————————————————————————————

Thriving Consequences of Developmental Assets: Succeeding in School

Percentage of youth reporting they get mostly A's on their report card.

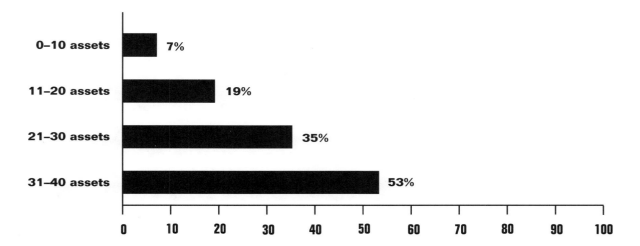

TABLE 4.13 —————————————————————————————————————

Succeeding in School, by Level of Assets, by Grade and Gender (in %)

LEVEL OF ASSETS		ALL	GRADE						
			6	7	8	9	10	11	12
0–10 assets	**All**	**7**	**10**	**8**	**8**	**6**	**5**	**7**	**9**
	Females	8	12	9	9	7	7	9	11
	Males	6	9	8	7	6	4	6	8
11–20 assets	**All**	**19**	**18**	**19**	**21**	**19**	**18**	**17**	**19**
	Females	21	19	22	24	20	20	19	22
	Males	17	17	17	19	18	16	15	16
21–30 assets	**All**	**35**	**29**	**35**	**38**	**36**	**35**	**36**	**39**
	Females	38	32	38	42	38	38	40	41
	Males	31	26	30	32	33	31	30	35
31–40 assets	**All**	**53**	**45**	**54**	**58**	**53**	**51**	**54**	**55**
	Females	56	49	57	62	56	57	57	60
	Males	45	38	49	49	45	38	48	45

FIGURE 4.14

Thriving Consequences of Developmental Assets: Helping Others

Percentage of youth reporting they help friends or neighbors one or more hours per week.

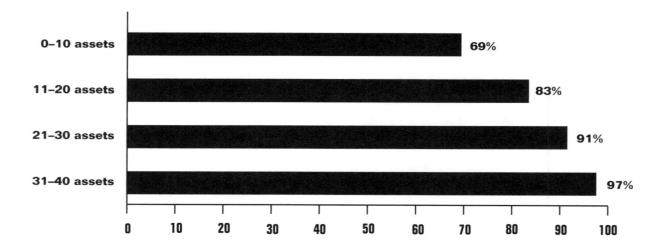

TABLE 4.14

Helping Others, by Level of Assets, by Grade and Gender (in %)

LEVEL OF ASSETS		ALL	GRADE						
			6	7	8	9	10	11	12
0–10 assets	All	69	67	66	66	69	69	71	70
	Females	75	71	74	73	76	77	76	72
	Males	65	64	62	61	64	64	69	69
11–20 assets	All	83	82	83	83	83	84	84	84
	Females	86	84	87	86	87	87	86	86
	Males	81	81	80	80	80	81	82	81
21–30 assets	All	91	91	90	91	90	91	91	90
	Females	92	93	91	93	92	93	91	91
	Males	89	88	89	90	87	89	90	88
31–40 assets	All	97	97	96	96	96	96	96	97
	Females	97	97	97	97	97	96	96	97
	Males	96	98	95	95	96	96	96	97

FIGURE 4.15

Thriving Consequences of Developmental Assets: Valuing Diversity

Percentage of youth reporting they place high importance on getting to know people of other racial and ethnic groups.

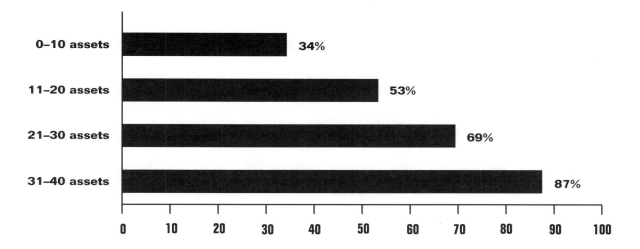

TABLE 4.15

Valuing Diversity, by Level of Assets, by Grade and Gender (in %)

LEVEL OF ASSETS		ALL	GRADE						
			6	7	8	9	10	11	12
0–10 assets	All	34	38	37	38	36	34	29	26
	Females	46	40	49	49	49	49	42	37
	Males	26	36	31	31	27	24	22	20
11–20 assets	All	53	55	55	55	54	51	50	50
	Females	62	61	62	65	64	62	60	59
	Males	44	50	50	46	43	40	39	41
21–30 assets	All	69	70	71	71	70	68	66	67
	Females	74	71	73	75	75	75	71	73
	Males	63	69	68	65	63	58	58	57
31–40 assets	All	87	88	88	85	86	86	84	86
	Females	88	90	90	87	89	87	86	88
	Males	83	84	85	80	82	84	78	83

FIGURE 4.16

Thriving Consequences of Developmental Assets: Maintaining Good Health

Percentage of youth reporting they pay attention to healthy nutrition and exercise.

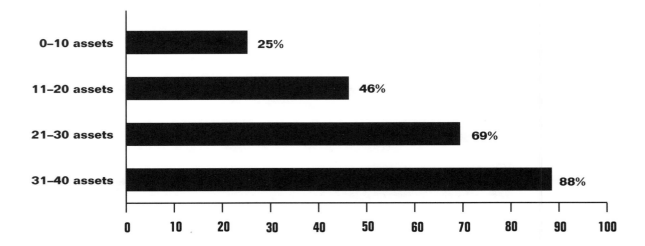

TABLE 4.16

Maintaining Good Health, by Level of Assets, by Grade and Gender (in %)

LEVEL OF ASSETS		ALL	GRADE						
			6	7	8	9	10	11	12
0–10 assets	**All**	**25**	**27**	**25**	**27**	**26**	**23**	**24**	**22**
	Females	22	25	23	26	22	19	20	18
	Males	27	28	27	28	29	25	26	24
11–20 assets	**All**	**46**	**47**	**47**	**49**	**47**	**46**	**43**	**41**
	Females	41	44	45	46	42	41	38	35
	Males	50	48	50	53	53	50	49	47
21–30 assets	**All**	**69**	**71**	**72**	**72**	**70**	**66**	**65**	**63**
	Females	66	71	70	70	67	63	61	58
	Males	73	71	75	74	75	72	71	70
31–40 assets	**All**	**88**	**92**	**91**	**90**	**87**	**86**	**83**	**78**
	Females	88	92	91	89	86	85	82	77
	Males	90	93	91	93	89	88	87	83

FIGURE 4.17

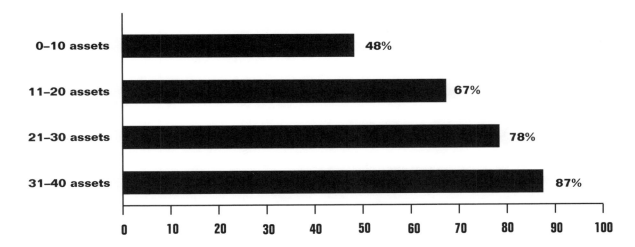

Thriving Consequences of Developmental Assets: Exhibiting Leadership

Percentage of youth reporting they have been a leader of a group or organization in the past 12 months.

TABLE 4.17

Exhibiting Leadership, by Level of Assets, by Grade and Gender (in %)

LEVEL OF ASSETS		ALL	GRADE						
			6	7	8	9	10	11	12
0–10 assets	All	48	48	48	49	48	46	49	52
	Females	46	47	43	47	44	45	49	49
	Males	49	49	51	50	50	46	49	53
11–20 assets	All	67	59	62	65	67	67	70	73
	Females	65	57	59	64	66	67	69	70
	Males	68	60	64	67	67	68	72	75
21–30 assets	All	78	70	72	76	79	82	86	87
	Females	78	70	71	75	79	82	86	87
	Males	79	71	73	77	79	81	85	88
31–40 assets	All	87	81	83	90	88	92	93	95
	Females	88	82	84	91	88	93	93	96
	Males	86	78	83	89	88	92	94	94

FIGURE 4.18

Thriving Consequences of Developmental Assets: Resisting Danger

Percentage of youth reporting they avoid doing things that are dangerous.

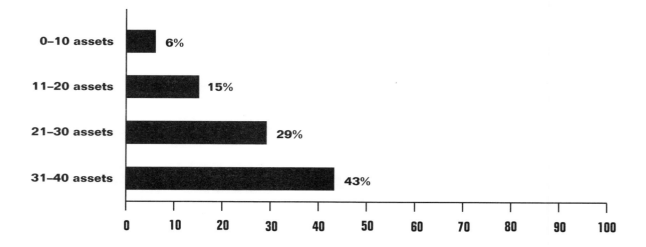

TABLE 4.18

Resisting Danger, by Level of Assets, by Grade and Gender (in %)

LEVEL OF ASSETS		ALL	GRADE						
			6	7	8	9	10	11	12
0–10 assets	All	6	8	8	6	6	6	7	6
	Females	8	10	11	6	7	7	8	8
	Males	6	8	7	5	5	5	6	5
11–20 assets	All	15	19	18	14	14	13	14	16
	Females	19	26	23	17	16	17	19	23
	Males	11	14	13	11	11	9	9	10
21–30 assets	All	29	36	31	28	26	26	28	29
	Females	34	42	37	32	31	32	35	35
	Males	21	28	24	22	19	17	19	19
31–40 assets	All	43	47	46	41	41	43	40	43
	Females	48	52	49	47	45	49	46	49
	Males	34	37	39	29	31	33	27	26

FIGURE 4.19

Thriving Consequences of Developmental Assets: Delaying Gratification

Percentage of youth reporting they save money for something special rather than spending it all right away.

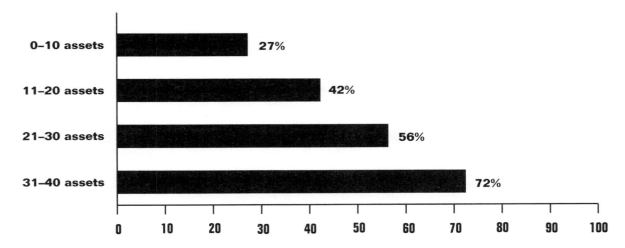

TABLE 4.19

Delaying Gratification, by Level of Assets, by Grade and Gender (in %)

LEVEL OF ASSETS		ALL	GRADE						
			6	7	8	9	10	11	12
0–10 assets	**All**	**27**	**30**	**28**	**26**	**27**	**25**	**28**	**28**
	Females	22	26	22	20	20	20	25	28
	Males	30	32	31	30	32	29	30	28
11–20 assets	**All**	**42**	**43**	**42**	**43**	**42**	**41**	**42**	**41**
	Females	37	39	37	37	36	36	39	39
	Males	46	46	46	48	48	47	44	43
21–30 assets	**All**	**56**	**56**	**59**	**58**	**55**	**54**	**55**	**54**
	Females	53	53	56	54	51	50	52	52
	Males	61	59	63	65	61	61	59	57
31–40 assets	**All**	**72**	**76**	**74**	**72**	**69**	**71**	**70**	**70**
	Females	71	74	74	71	67	69	65	69
	Males	76	79	75	75	75	76	80	74

FIGURE 4.20

Thriving Consequences of Developmental Assets: Overcoming Adversity

Percentage of youth reporting they do not give up when things get difficult.

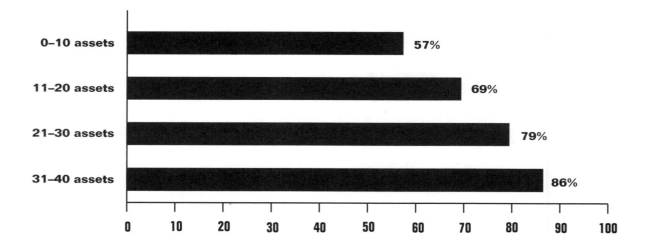

TABLE 4.20

Overcoming Adversity, by Level of Assets, by Grade and Gender (in %)

LEVEL OF ASSETS		ALL	GRADE						
			6	7	8	9	10	11	12
0–10 assets	All	57	57	57	56	56	56	58	61
	Females	50	54	52	50	49	48	50	51
	Males	61	58	59	60	61	61	63	66
11–20 assets	All	69	65	65	68	70	71	71	73
	Females	65	60	61	63	65	66	66	68
	Males	74	69	69	73	74	76	77	77
21–30 assets	All	79	74	75	77	81	82	83	85
	Females	78	73	74	77	80	80	82	82
	Males	81	75	77	78	82	85	85	89
31–40 assets	All	86	80	86	85	88	89	91	92
	Females	87	81	87	85	88	89	91	91
	Males	85	78	84	84	87	88	91	94

The Resiliency Power of Developmental Assets ———

Resiliency is an area of inquiry and practice grounded in a growing legacy of scientific research.[2] Resiliency enables us to beat the odds and build healthy lives in the face of hardship, trauma, or adversity. In the words of one of the preeminent researchers in this field, Emmy Werner, resilience describes three phenomena: "good developmental outcomes despite high-risk status, sustained competence under stress, and recovery from trauma."[3]

Resiliency researchers focus attention on identifying individual, family, and community factors that help young people beat the odds.[4] The framework of developmental assets draws heavily on this research. For example, Table 4.21 shows how some of the keys to resiliency directly tie in to one or more of the 40 developmental assets. Thus, we would expect our data to show some of the same positive impact of these factors as has been found by other researchers.

Do the developmental assets help young people be resilient, beat the odds, or cope well with stress? Do they help ameliorate the negative impact of adversity?

To examine these questions, we can look at the effect of assets on young people who are faced with the five developmental deficits discussed in Chapter 3 and measured in our survey of 6th- to 12th-grade youth. We created an index of the five developmental deficits (i.e., alone at home, TV overexposure, physical abuse, victim of violence, and drinking parties). Of the 99,462 youth surveyed, 4,063 reported having all five of these deficits simultaneously. By focusing on this smaller group of highly vulnerable youth, we can look at whether these young people are better off if they have more assets in their lives—whether the assets help them beat the odds that seem to be stacked against them.

We can see the impact of assets in the lives of these highly vulnerable youth in two ways. First, as shown in Figure 4.21, highly vulnerable youth report engaging in fewer patterns of high-risk behavior (as described in Chapter 3 and earlier in this chapter) if they experience more assets. Vulnerable youth who also experience 31 or more of the assets engage, on average, in just 2 of the 10 patterns of high-risk behavior. In contrast, vulnerable youth who experience few assets (0-10) engage in an average of 6.1 of the 10 high-risk behavior patterns.

[2] See, for example, N. Garmezy, "The Study of Competence in Children at Risk for Severe Psychopathology," in E.J. Anthony and C. Koupernik (eds.), *The Child and His Family: Vol. 3. Children at Psychiatric Risk* (pp. 77-97) (New York: Wiley, 1974); M. Rutter, "Protective Factors in Children's Response to Stress and Disadvantage," in W. M. Kent and J. E. Rolf (eds.), *Primary Prevention of Psychology* (Vol. 3, pp. 49-74) (Hanover, NH: University Press of New England, 1979); E. E. Werner and R. S. Smith, *Overcoming the Odds: High Risk Children from Birth to Adulthood* (Ithaca, NY: Cornell University Press, 1992).

[3] Emmy E. Werner, "Resilience in Development." *Current Directions in Psychological Science, 4,* no. 3 (1995), 81.

[4] For a review of the literature on resiliency, see Byron Egeland, Deborah Jacobvitz, and L. Alan Sroufe, "Breaking the Cycle of Abuse," *Child Development, 59* (August 1988), 1080-1088; Norman Garmezy, "Resilience and Vulnerability to Adverse Developmental Outcomes Associated with Poverty," *American Behavioral Scientist, 34* (1991), 416-430; and Ann S. Masten, Karin M. Best, and Norman Garmezy, "Resilience and Development: Contributions from the Study of Children Who Overcome Adversity," *Development and Psychopathology,* 2 (4) (1990), 425-444.

TABLE 4.21

Ties between Resiliency Research and Developmental Assets

SELECTED KEYS TO RESILIENCY, AS IDENTIFIED BY OTHER RESEARCHERS	CONNECTIONS TO THE 40 DEVELOPMENTAL ASSETS
Social competence (e.g., empathy, caring, communication skills)	#26: Caring #33: Interpersonal competence
Caring, attentive family environments	#1: Family support #2: Positive family communication #11: Family boundaries
Surrogate caregivers (extended family members, siblings, unrelated adults) who provide counsel, safety, and support, particularly when parent or parents are absent or inattentive	#3: Other adult relationships #4: Caring neighborhood #13: Neighborhood boundaries #14: Adult role models #15: Positive peer influence
Academic success	#21: Achievement motivation #22: School engagement #23: Homework #24: Bonding to school
Youth participation in school and community-based programs	#17: Creative activities #18: Youth programs #19: Religious community
Healthy self-concept and a sense of personal efficacy or control over one's environment	#37: Personal power #38: Self-esteem
High expectations	#16: High expectations
Assignment of productive roles and responsibility in family or community life	#8: Youth as resources #9: Service to others

We see the same kind of impact in Table 4.22, which shows the percentages of vulnerable youth who report engaging in zero, one, or multiple high-risk behavior patterns as a function of their levels of assets. For example, one-third of the vulnerable youth with 31-40 assets are engaged in none of the high-risk behavior patterns, despite the fact that they experience all five of the deficits. In contrast, only 1 percent of the vulnerable, low-asset youth (10 or fewer assets) engage in none of the high-risk behavior patterns. In fact, almost half of the low-asset youth who also experience all five deficits engage in seven or more of the high-risk behavior patterns.

FIGURE 4.21

Average Number of High-Risk Behavior Patterns among Vulnerable Youth, by Level of Assets*

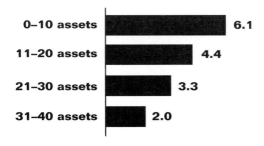

0–10 assets	6.1
11–20 assets	4.4
21–30 assets	3.3
31–40 assets	2.0

* N = 4,063 6th- to 12th-grade students who report simultaneously experiencing the five developmental deficits: alone at home, TV overexposure, physical abuse, victim of violence, and drinking parties; a subsample from the aggregate sample of 99,462 who took the *Search Institute Profiles of Student Life: Attitudes and Behaviors* survey during the 1996-97 school year.

TABLE 4.22

Vulnerable Adolescents' Reports of Engagement in High-Risk Behavior Patterns as a Function of Asset Level*

PERCENTAGE WHO REPORT ENGAGING IN HIGH-RISK BEHAVIOR PATTERNS . . .	NUMBER OF 10 HIGH-RISK BEHAVIOR PATTERNS REPORTED (%)										
	0	1	2	3	4	5	6	7	8	9	10
IF 0–10 ASSETS	1	3	6	7	11	13	13	16	15	10	5
IF 11–20 ASSETS	5	10	15	15	12	12	11	9	5	5	1
IF 21–30 ASSETS	11	20	19	15	12	9	7	4	1	0	0
IF 31–40 ASSETS	33	29	13	13	0	8	0	4	0	0	0

* N = 4,063 6th- to 12th-grade students who report simultaneously experiencing the five developmental deficits: alone at home, TV overexposure, physical abuse, victim of violence, and drinking parties; a subsample from the aggregate sample of 99,462 who took the *Search Institute Profiles of Student Life: Attitudes and Behaviors* survey during the 1996-97 school year.

The Power of Assets for Vulnerable Youth

Asset building is effective for all youth, not just youth with a lot already going well in their lives. In fact, the more vulnerable youth are, the more they seem to benefit from the protective impact of developmental assets.

Figure 4.22 shows that the more deficits youth have, the greater the protective power of the assets. The percentages represent youth who do not engage in any of the 10 high-risk behavior patterns, suggesting that they are making healthy life choices. We can also see that young people with high asset levels are consistently more likely to avoid these high-risk behaviors than are those with average levels of assets. But most important is that the differences between high-asset and average-asset youth are most pronounced among those who experience the most deficits. For example, high-asset youth experiencing all five deficits are more than seven times as likely as average-asset youth experiencing all five deficits to avoid all the high-risk behavior patterns. In contrast, those high-asset youth who experience none of these deficits are less than twice as likely as average-asset youth to avoid all the high-risk behavior patterns. Thus, having a high number of assets is particularly powerful for youth who live the challenge of many deficits.

FIGURE 4.22

Average-Asset and High-Asset Youth with No Risk Patterns, by Asset Level and Deficits (in %)

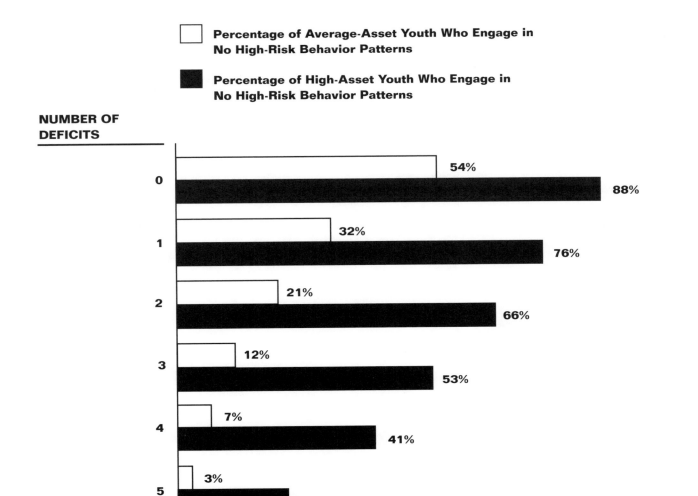

☐ Percentage of Average-Asset Youth Who Engage in No High-Risk Behavior Patterns

■ Percentage of High-Asset Youth Who Engage in No High-Risk Behavior Patterns

NUMBER OF DEFICITS

0	54% / 88%
1	32% / 76%
2	21% / 66%
3	12% / 53%
4	7% / 41%
5	3% / 23%

0 10 20 30 40 50 60 70 80 90 100

Average-Asset Youth = Youth with 11–20 developmental assets.
High-Asset Youth = Youth with 31–40 developmental assets.

Resilience in the Face of Specific Deficits ———————

Table 4.23 looks at each of the developmental deficits, showing how the average number of risk patterns youth engage in decreases as the number of assets increases. For each deficit, we see that young people with the most assets engage in the fewest high-risk behavior patterns. For example, high-asset youth who have been victims of violence on average engage in fewer than one of the 10 high-risk behavior patterns. In contrast, youth who have been victims of violence but have 10 or fewer assets engage in an average of 5.2 of the 10 high-risk behavior patterns.

Young people who experience each of the deficits are more likely to report the thriving indicators if they have higher levels of assets (Table 4.24). For example, high-asset youth who experience the alone-at-home deficit have, on average, 6 of the 8 thriving indicators, compared to 2.7 thriving indicators for low-asset youth with the same deficit. Thus, despite the challenges they face, youth with many assets manage not only to avoid more of the negative behaviors but also to engage in more of the positive ones.

TABLE 4.23

Average Number of High-Risk Behavior Patterns
by Level of Assets for Each Deficit

DEFICIT	AVERAGE NUMBER OF 10 HIGH-RISK BEHAVIOR PATTERNS FOR EACH LEVEL OF ASSETS			
	0–10 Assets	11–20 Assets	21–30 Assets	31–40 Assets
Alone at home	4.7	2.7	1.2	.4
TV overexposure	4.4	2.4	1.1	.4
Physical abuse	5.0	2.9	1.4	.6
Victim of violence	5.2	3.2	1.6	.7
Drinking parties	5.2	3.3	1.8	.8

TABLE 4.24

Average Number of Thriving Indicators
by Level of Assets for Each Deficit

DEFICIT	AVERAGE NUMBER OF 10 THRIVING INDICATORS FOR EACH LEVEL OF ASSETS			
	0–10 Assets	11–20 Assets	21–30 Assets	31–40 Assets
Alone at home	2.7	3.9	5.0	6.0
TV overexposure	2.6	3.8	4.8	5.9
Physical abuse	2.8	4.0	5.0	6.0
Victim of violence	2.8	4.0	5.0	6.0
Drinking parties	2.8	4.0	5.1	5.9

Summary on the Overall Impact of Developmental Assets

This chapter has explored the relationship between developmental assets and high-risk behaviors, their impact on thriving outcomes, and their role in helping young people be resilient in the face of adversity. And while our data do not demonstrate a cause-effect relationship, other research in adolescent development, resiliency, and prevention gives us confidence that these relations point to the powerful impact that assets can have in young people's lives. The assets reduce risk, increase thriving, and strengthen resilience.

Preventing risky behavior

The impact of assets on high-risk behavior patterns is dramatic, as shown in Table 4.25. For example, youth with 31 to 40 assets are less likely to abuse alcohol (3 percent vs. 30 percent), less likely to use tobacco (1 percent vs. 21 percent), and less likely to engage in antisocial behavior (7 percent vs. 23 percent) than youth with average levels of assets (11-20).

Promoting thriving

Although the effects of the assets on thriving indicators are not as dramatic, high-asset youth still are much more likely than average-asset youth to report having each of the eight thriving indicators (Table 4.26).

Increasing resiliency

Youth with 31 to 40 assets are less likely to report engaging in three or more high-risk behavior patterns at each level of developmental deficits than youth with 11 to 20 assets (average-asset youth). In other words, even facing similar deficits in their lives as other youth, those with the most assets are far more resilient and less likely to report engaging in risky behaviors. For example, among all youth with three deficits, 52 percent of average-asset youth engage in three or more high-risk behavior patterns, compared with only 7 percent of high-asset youth.

We see a similar pattern for thriving indicators: At every level of deficits, youth with 31 to 40 assets are more likely to report having six or more of the eight thriving indicators than youth with just an average number of assets.

From all these perspectives, then, the value of adding asset-building efforts to the mix of what individuals, organizations, and communities do for and with youth is clear.

TABLE 4.25

The Impact of Assets on Average-Asset versus High-Asset Youth Engaged in High-Risk Behavior Patterns and Affected by Deficits (in %)

Youth Engaging in Patterns of High-Risk Behaviors	Average-Asset Youth (11–20 Assets)	High-Asset Youth (31–40 Assets)
Problem alcohol use	30	3
Tobacco use	21	1
Illicit drug use	19	1
Sexual intercourse	21	3
Depression and suicide	25	4
Antisocial behavior	23	7
Violence	35	6
School problems	19	2
Driving and alcohol	24	4
Gambling	23	6
Youth Reporting at Least Three Patterns of High-Risk Behaviors, by Number of Deficits Experienced		
0	8	<1
1	27	1
2	39	4
3	52	7
4	65	16
5	74	33

TABLE 4.26

The Impact of Assets on Average-Asset versus High-Asset Youth Engaged in Thriving Behaviors and Affected by Deficits (in %)

Youth Engaging in Thriving Indicators	Average-Asset Youth (11–20 Assets)	High-Asset Youth (31–40 Assets)
Succeeds in school	19	53
Helps others	83	97
Values diversity	53	87
Maintains good health	46	88
Exhibits leadership	57	87
Resists danger	15	43
Delays gratification	42	72
Overcomes adversity	69	86
Youth with at Least Six Thriving Indicators, by Number of Deficits Experienced		
0	14	79
1	13	71
2	12	68
3	11	63
4	11	61
5	11	58

Assets Are Powerful, But Not a Guarantee

The assets clearly have protective, enhancing, and resiliency consequences in the lives of adolescents. It might also be true that the assets have longer-term consequences, predicting how successful one is as a parent, a worker, a citizen. Research is needed to track these long-term indicators of developmental assets.

It is important to emphasize that the power of the assets comes through their accumulation, not by identifying the one or two things that make the difference. Across all different roles that assets appear to play in promoting healthy development during adolescence, the consistent theme is that the assets are additive or cumulative. The more the better. Ideally, all young people will experience 31 or more of the 40 assets. Yet, as noted in Chapter 2, only 8 percent of youth experience this level of assets. Sixty-two percent experience 20 or fewer of the 40 assets.

It is also important to point out that these data are descriptive in nature, and there are therefore inherent limitations to these findings. We emphasize that:

1. **Assets are not a cure-all.** Increasing the number of assets young people experience increases the odds that they will thrive; it doesn't guarantee it. Some youth with the highest levels of assets still engage in patterns of high-risk behavior. Other factors—genetics, temperament, traumas, and a host of other possible individual differences—also influence young people's behavior.

2. **Circumstances do not entirely determine destiny.** Living with high levels of deficits, living in poverty, living in a violent environment, living with an abusive or addicted parent can all make it more difficult for young people to thrive. But some do, particularly when they experience positive, reinforcing relationships, opportunities,

and personal qualities such as those identified in the 40 assets. So while we can and should work toward changing the harmful circumstances in young people's lives, we do not have to wait for those changes to occur before we take positive action that promises to make a lasting difference. Building assets can improve the odds that all young people, regardless of their circumstances, can grow up healthy, caring, and responsible.

3. **A lack of assets does not make failure inevitable.** Some young people with few assets do not engage in any of the high-risk behaviors. Some are resilient despite the lack of these positive reinforcers in their lives. Again, other factors also play a role in shaping young people's lives and choices.

4. **Engaging in risky behaviors does not inevitably lead to dire consequences.** Many people who engage in harmful activities early in life grow into responsible, contributing members of families, communities, and society. Those experiences may leave scars, but they do not necessarily spiral downward into more and more negative patterns.

In short, developmental assets are powerful, but human development is a complex process that involves many factors and influences. There are no guarantees. That does not mean, however, that nothing can be done to improve the lives of young people. Building assets is about doing the positive things that make it more likely that young people—in all circumstances and facing many different challenges—will not only survive, but thrive, through and beyond childhood and adolescence.

5

Building a Solid Foundation for Healthy Development

This report has explored several major dimensions of adolescent development and well-being. In Chapter 2, we focused on young people's experiences of developmental assets. In Chapter 3, we examined their experiences of developmental deficits and patterns of high-risk behaviors. Chapter 4 looked at thriving indicators and explored the connections between assets and the other dimensions. This chapter seeks to draw all of this information together to help portray the challenges and opportunities before us in building a solid, lasting foundation for the young people in our families, neighborhoods, schools, congregations, organizations, and communities.

To do this, we present a picture of what we mean by healthy, thriving young people to use as a measuring stick to assess our current situation. Then we point to the kinds of comprehensive strategies needed that hold promise for creating a healthier future for all young people.

Building Blocks of a Solid Foundation

To provide a starting point, we propose that healthy, thriving young people—those on a positive developmental path—would have all of the following elements of overall well-being:

- 31 or more of the 40 assets;

- 1 or none of the 5 deficits;

- 2 or fewer of the 10 high-risk behavior patterns; and

- at least 6 of the 8 thriving indicators.

At some level, the specific target numbers are somewhat arbitrary, although this represents a common method for understanding data.[1] Furthermore, meeting the criteria would not guarantee that all young people avoided all harm or that they would all be highly successful in life. But having these building blocks profoundly increases the odds that most youth would have a much better chance of living up to all their potential.

If these criteria represent a worthwhile goal, then Figure 5.1 shows the extent of our challenge: *Less than 4 percent of youth report experiencing that level of overall well-being.* In addition, females are more likely than males to report meeting the overall well-being criteria; and while the percentage of youth meeting the wellness criteria is 9 percent in 6th grade, it is just 2 percent in 12th grade.

---

[1] The definitions of all four dimensions represent our attempt to use a common method of dividing a variable into quartiles: Youth with more than 75% of the assets (more than 30), and at least 6 of the 8 thriving indicators are in the top quartile of that variable's total possible score. The 5 developmental deficits and 10 risk behavior patterns do not divide neatly into quartiles, and so those standards were set at 1 of 5 deficits (the top 20%), and 2 of 10 risk behavior patterns (20%). To allow those cutoff points to be higher (i.e., 2 of 5 deficits, or 40%, and 3 of 10 risk patterns, or 30%) would have been too lenient a criterion for overall wellness, a status representing an ideal for youth development toward which we should aspire.

FIGURE 5.1

Youth Reporting Overall Well-Being, by Gender and Grade

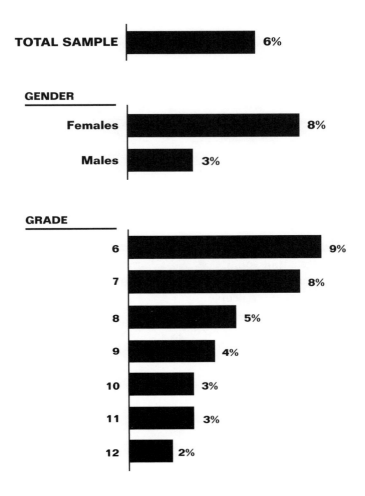

TOTAL SAMPLE — 6%

GENDER
Females — 8%
Males — 3%

GRADE
6 — 9%
7 — 8%
8 — 5%
9 — 4%
10 — 3%
11 — 3%
12 — 2%

Are the Criteria Too High?

If just one in 20 young people reports meeting the proposed well-being criteria, are these standards simply unrealistic? The data suggest that they are not.

If we look at the problems in young people's lives, the goals are not far from the current situation, as shown in Table 5.1. The average young person surveyed reports a little less than two of the deficits, so one or none is not a terribly stringent goal. Furthermore, the average young person reports a little more than two risk patterns, so achieving a standard of two or fewer for all youth seems reasonable.

The gap between actual and ideal is much larger when we look at the positives. Only 8 percent of young people surveyed report 31 to 40 assets, and the average youth has only about 18. And, finally, young people report having an average of little more than half of the thriving indicators. Is it not appropriate to want all youth to have more positive behaviors and outcomes?

Another way to address the issue is to ask: If we lower our expectations, what are we really communicating? In which areas—deficits, risks, assets, thriving behaviors—would we want less for our young people? Even if we relaxed our standards so that two or three times as many youth met the criteria, a majority of youth still would not do so.

To us, the problem is not definitional but a real, pressing challenge facing our families, communities, and nation. That challenge is to discover how we will work to build a stronger foundation for all young people.

TABLE 5.1

Actual versus Desired Level of Each Element of Youth Well-Being

	DESIRED	ACTUAL*		
		Total Sample	6th Graders	12th Graders
Deficits (out of 5)	2.0	1.9	1.5	2.0
High-risk behavior patterns (out of 10)	2.0	2.2	1.2	3.0
Developmental assets (out of 40)	31.0	18.8	21.5	17.2
Thriving indicators (out of 8)	6.0	4.2	4.5	4.0

*Average number of deficits, high-risk patterns, developmental assets, and thriving indicators reported by 99,462 6th- to 12th-grade youth surveyed during the 1996-97 school year.

What Is Preventing Us from Strengthening the Foundation?

What in our culture contributes to the current situation, in which only a small minority of young people have in place all the elements of a solid foundation for healthy development? A full analysis is beyond the scope of this report.[2] However, we propose the following as some of the factors:

- Adult silence about boundaries, values, and expectations;

- The fragmentation of and competition among many socializing systems;

- Age segregation and the general disengagement of the public from building meaningful connections with youth;

- High levels of parental absence in the lives of children;

- The isolation of people of all ages within neighborhoods;

- Overexposure to the mass media without critical examination of its messages and images;

- Barriers to healthy development such as poverty, lack of access to programs and services, and families without the skills and support to care for their children;

- Adult fear of involvement and a sense that youth are the responsibility of "someone else" or, conversely, the responsibility of just parents or guardians; and

- Schools, religious institutions, and other youth-serving organizations that are not adequately equipped to be sources of support, caring, and positive challenge.

This combination of factors suggests, among other things, that our communities are not places where caring, connectedness, and a shared sense of purpose are common or where a commitment to children dominates public and private life. It also reminds us that no single part of society is solely to blame for the current state of affairs—not schools, not families, not the media. Rather, all elements of our culture share in the responsibility for what has gone wrong as well as the responsibility for making more things go right.

[2] A more detailed analysis is found in Peter L. Benson, *All Kids Are Our Kids: What Communities Must Do to Raise Caring and Responsible Children and Adolescents* (San Francisco: Jossey-Bass, 1997).

Creating Healthy Communities for Youth

In order to strengthen young people's foundation for healthy development, multiple strategies converge into a vision of healthy communities for youth—communities in which all residents, organizations, networks, and institutions work together on behalf of children and youth. Building a strong foundation for all youth calls for valuing and holding in creative tension several seemingly competing themes:

A positive focus *and* A problem-reduction focus

Family and organizational commitment *and* Community-wide commitment

Comprehensive strategies *and* Targeted strategies

Informal asset building *and* Formal asset building

All youth *and* Individual differences

Focus on children *and* Focus on adolescents

A Positive Focus

The developmental assets highlight the critical need to dedicate energy, creativity, commitment, and resources to basic, positive elements of human development:

- Having caring relationships with each other;

- Sharing and passing on our values;

- Articulating and enforcing appropriate boundaries;

- Providing opportunities to contribute to the common good;

- Having positive, enriching ways to spend time; and

- Nurturing the skills, commitments, and perspectives that shape character.

The list could be much longer, naming all of the 40 assets as well as other life-enriching qualities. But if the young people whose experiences are reported here are any indicator, the gaps in each of these experiences are signals that we have neglected these basic, relationship-based socializing experiences in our communities.

Paying attention to these positive experiences—identified and measured in the 40 assets—has implications for all levels of communities and society. For example:

- *Youth, adults, and families* will be more intentional about nurturing caring, positive relationships and experiences for young people, not waiting for serious problems to erupt before getting involved in the lives of children and youth. Neighbors, friends, extended family, and acquaintances will all discover the ways in which they can and do contribute to young people's assets.

- *Organizations and institutions* in communities—schools, government agencies, law enforcement, congregations, youth organizations, social service agencies, businesses, and others—will examine their own practices to better align their efforts with the vision of asset building.

- *Whole communities* will explore ways to work together to ensure that all areas of community life offer asset-building strength for all young people.

- In time, leaders and institutions that shape *society's norms and priorities,* from policy makers to the media, will discover how their influence can be used in positive ways to create an environment that reinforces and encourages asset building.

Complementing Problem-Reduction Strategies ——

An emphasis on asset building does not mean we should abandon problem-reduction or intervention strategies. Indeed, no single strategy, approach, program, or model will, by itself, shore up the fragile foundation upon which our young people now build their lives. In addition to asset building, communities must also engage in:

- **Risk reduction,** which provides formal and directed programs to the young people who are at risk of experiencing problems; and

- **Intervention and treatment programs,** which provide specialized help for youth who already are experiencing difficulties.

Each strategy has an impact on the success of the other strategies. As Figure 5.2 shows, asset building is the broadest foundational approach, focusing on promoting positive building blocks of success among *all* youth. To the extent that communities succeed in helping their youth experience a high average level of assets, the community's risk-reduction and treatment efforts are likely to be affected as well. There may be less need for those strategies, or the population of youth that needs these more intensive services may be smaller, in asset-rich environments with a strong economic infrastructure.

FIGURE 5.2 ——————————————————————————————

Complementary Approaches to Increasing Youth Well-Being

Individual and Organizational Commitment ————

One of the most important concepts in thinking about developmental assets is the value of having all parts of young people's lives be asset rich. While a supportive and loving family life gives young people an advantage, that advantage is weakened if those same youth have poor school experiences and do not have meaningful relationships and structured time in their community.

Table 5.2 illustrates this point. We selected four assets to represent contexts that play key roles in many young people's lives: family (asset #1—family support), school (asset #5—positive school climate), youth programs (asset #18), and religious community (asset #19).

Young people who have all four of these context-specific assets are much less likely than youth with fewer or none of these four assets to engage in any of the risk patterns. For example, as can be seen in the table, youth with none of these assets are *five times* more likely to experience depression and suicide attempts than youth with all four of these assets (43 percent vs. 8 percent). Thus, ensuring that young people have supportive families, positive school climates, and access to involvement in structured activities in youth programs and congregations is likely to help young people avoid risky behavior and to experience healthy development.

TABLE 5.2 ————————————————————————————

Youth Who Report Engagement in High-Risk Behavior Patterns, by Number of Context-Specific Assets Experienced (in %)*

	0 Assets	1 Asset	2 Assets	3 Assets	4 Assets
Problem alcohol use	48	37	27	19	11
Tobacco use	46	30	18	10	5
Illicit drug use	41	28	17	10	5
Sexual intercourse	36	26	18	11	8
Depression and suicide	43	32	23	14	8
Antisocial behavior	45	32	23	14	8
Violence	53	43	34	25	16
School problems	44	30	18	11	5
Driving and alcohol	39	30	22	15	10
Gambling	28	24	22	18	14

*The following external assets were selected to represent four contexts that play a key role in many young people's lives: Family (asset #1, family support), school (asset #5, positive school climate), youth programs (asset #18, youth programs), and congregations (asset #19, religious community).

Community-wide Commitment

One danger in reporting on the power of the assets representing four contexts in young people's lives is giving the impression that a caring family and some youth programs are all that young people need. Why worry about all the other assets? Why not just focus on those four areas of young people's lives? It certainly would be much easier.

Yes, it might be easier, but the impact would be much less. Although the redundancy of positive experiences in the four contexts is valuable, this power does not match the effect we see from *all* 40 assets. For the example of depression/suicide, youth with 0 to 10 assets are 10 times more likely to experience depression and/or suicide than youth with 31 to 40 assets (40 percent versus 4 percent). (See Table 4.5 in Chapter 4.)

In other words, youth who have 31 to 40 assets appear to be protected against depression and suicide, more so than even those fortunate youth who have assets in each of four important environments in their lives. The whole set of 40 assets has even greater protective power for the other high-risk patterns.

This finding underscores the importance of both the *distribution* and the *number* of assets. Youth who experience a handful of key assets everywhere they turn are indeed more protected from risk than other youth. But we must resist the temptation to focus only on that smaller number of assets, because youth who experience a majority of the 40 assets in all areas of their lives are much more likely to thrive.

Comprehensive Strategies

Whether the focus is on assets, risks, thriving, or deficits, it is important to remember that young people do not experience one asset, one risk behavior, one deficit, or one thriving indicator in isolation from the others. Like the strands in a spider's web, these experiences—whether positive or negative—have an impact on each other, all being moved when one part is touched.

Whether a community's primary goal is to reduce risks or promote thriving, the multiple and co-occurring relationships among risky and positive behaviors call on us to use strategies that address multiple issues at once, not just a select few. As seen in Chapter 3, the high-risk behavior patterns tend to co-occur; that is, if young people engage in one of the risk patterns, they are several times more likely to engage in other risk patterns as well. Thus, trying to deal only with one problem while ignoring others is less likely to have an impact long term.

The same kind of co-occurrence is evident with the thriving indicators. Youth who have one of the thriving indicators also are more likely to have other thriving indicators, especially to be physically healthy, demonstrate leadership, and achieve success at school. Helping youth thrive in one way raises the chances of their thriving in other ways, too. Therefore, collaboration across all community sectors is not just a nice way of thinking about community; it is essential if we want to tap into the interlocking power of both risks and thriving behaviors. And it is possible.

Targeted Strategies

Building assets can lessen risks and promote thriving among all youth. But where special risk or failure to thrive exists, more targeted risk-reduction efforts and focused promotion of positive behaviors are essential.

Targeted risk-reduction strategies are also important because not all risk patterns are equally powerful; some risk patterns seem to have particularly strong influences on the chances of youth engaging in *other* high-risk behavior patterns. For example, the following high-risk behavior patterns seem to have a pervasive negative effect:

- All of the substance use risk patterns;

- Engaging in sexual intercourse three or more times;

- Engaging in antisocial behavior; and

- Violence.

Each of these risk patterns increases the odds that youth will engage in other risk patterns as well. Given the negative influences of these high-risk behavior patterns, building up the protective factors and assets in young people's lives cannot alone ensure young people's well-being. Focused efforts that try to reduce those particular risk behaviors are a critical part of the total community response.

Informal Asset Building

Most of the efforts to improve the well-being of children and adolescents in recent decades have focused on formal, structured programs, usually targeted at reducing or eliminating a particular problem. While these kinds of targeted interventions are important, the 40 developmental assets underscore the importance of informal, individual acts of caring and commitment that, when added together, become the building blocks in a solid foundation upon which young people base their lives.

Most of the assets are built informally, the result of everyday acts of caring, support, relationship, and modeling. They are the result of what we do with, for, and about youth as neighbors, friends, coworkers, volunteers, and family members. They are the result of our being intentional about breaking the ice by saying hello to a teenager, demonstrating how to deal with conflict peacefully, asking young people to help us in doing something for someone in need, and myriad other interactions.

We can integrate asset-building topics into curricula and formalize them in programs in an effort to pass along these positive experiences. But young people are less likely to internalize these lessons if they do not experience such positive influences each and every day in their homes, neighborhoods, and other places where they spend time.

Formal Asset Building

While we emphasize the informal aspects of asset building (because they are easily neglected), there are also important roles for formal programmatic efforts to build assets.

The importance of institution-based asset building has been illustrated in a study that examined healthy communities, those in which overall youth risk pattern statistics are relatively low. In those communities, even vulnerable youth who do not have many assets report engaging in fewer risky behaviors than similarly vulnerable youth in less healthy communities.[3] When we examined some of the reasons why, we found that both vulnerable and less vulnerable youth in those healthy communities were more connected to their schools, more involved in after-school clubs and programs, and more involved with religious organizations than youth in less healthy communities.

In another analysis, we examined what "predicted" or explained six of the thriving indicators that we report on here, and found similar results. The time youth spend in youth programs sponsored by school or community organizations helped to explain five of the thriving indicators: succeeding in school, exhibiting leadership, maintaining health, helping others, and overcoming adversity.[4]

These findings and others like them underscore the importance of the formal efforts to build assets through existing youth-serving institutions. Contacts beyond those in the family provide critical opportunities for young people to be in relationships with caring and principled peers and adults, to have safe, structured places to spend time, and to develop internal values, skills, and commitments.

---

[3] Dale A. Blyth and Nancy Leffert, "Communities as Contexts for Adolescent Development: An Empirical Analysis," *Journal of Adolescent Research, 10* (1995), 64-87.

[4] Peter C. Scales, Peter L. Benson, Nancy Leffert, and Dale A. Blyth (in press), "The Strength of Developmental Assets as Predictors of Positive Youth Development Outcomes," *Applied Developmental Science.*

All Youth

Throughout this report, we have emphasized that asset building is important for all youth, regardless of their age, gender, race/ethnicity, type of family, type of community, or level of income. While there are important differences across demographic groups (discussed in detail in Appendixes A-D), the differences do not overshadow the central messages: All young people benefit from having assets in their lives, and virtually all young people, regardless of background, have too few.

In an age of limited time and money, it can be tempting to focus our asset-building efforts on certain subpopulations of youth—either those who "need it the most" or those who are most accessible. This strategy may be an adequate starting point, but we must keep in mind the vision of all young people having more assets.

Why is this broad focus so important? First, targeted strategies can label young people as "at risk" or otherwise different from other young people, thereby potentially marginalizing them. Second, a broad focus emphasizes that asset building unites all elements or sectors of the community in a shared perspective and priority. This shared understanding can reduce the finger-pointing that sometimes occurs when efforts focus only on particular groups of young people. Finally, young people have a powerful influence on each other, so working to build the asset base for all young people positively influences those who may be most vulnerable.

Individual Differences

This report has emphasized overall patterns in young people's assets, deficits, risky behaviors, and thriving. And while we have made some broad comparisons between genders and among youth of different races, residences, and family and socioeconomic backgrounds, we have also emphasized that no group of young people is either immune from the challenges or destined for a particular outcome because of its circumstances.

These general statements and analyses are important for understanding trends and patterns. However, a vast array of individual differences exists in real life that creates additional complexity. For example, individual differences among youth are critical in affecting assets. The timing of puberty, one's physical attractiveness, a certain level of intelligence, and a variety of temperamental characteristics—all biologically influenced—can affect, positively or negatively, young people's different experience of environments that may seem relatively similar.

In addition, this report suggests some areas where differences are likely to occur. We know, for example,

that females experience the assets somewhat differently than do males. We know that older youth are less likely to experience assets than younger youth. And we know that youth from some racial/ethnic backgrounds (such as African American) are more likely to experience assets than are youth from other groups (such as American Indian). These differences must be interpreted within the context of a deep understanding of the cultures involved, as well as the specific dynamics different groups of young people may face in this culture.

In short, as asset-building efforts address individual youth, it is important to understand the realities in these young people's lives. While statistics from nearly 100,000 young people might suggest issues to explore and options to consider, a young person's own experiences, background, temperament, personality, and other variables will shape how best to ensure that he or she will thrive.

Focus on Children

The report has also presented the data on 6th- to 12th-grade youth as if these youth existed independently of their younger selves. However, development during childhood has an impact on developmental success in adolescence. For example, cuddly and affectionate infants make their caregivers smile, and consequently receive more care and support than temperamental infants. In later childhood, that early support often translates into greater social skills and a greater ability to attract ongoing adult support. In turn, that social competence and ongoing support have been related to school success as adolescents.[5]

What we do for adolescents builds on what we do for younger children. Each developmental period lays the groundwork for the life experiences that follow. Therefore, a community that cares for and about its youth must at the same time provide the necessary healthy environment for its infants and young children, who will become tomorrow's youth.[6]

---

[5] Emmy E. Werner and Ruth S. Smith, *Overcoming the Odds: High Risk Children from Birth to Adulthood* (Ithaca, NY: Cornell University Press, 1992).

[6] For an exploration of developmental assets for younger children, see Nancy Leffert, Peter L. Benson, and Jolene L. Roehlkepartain, *Starting Out Right: Developmental Assets for Children* (Minneapolis: Search Institute, 1997).

Focus on Adolescents

A call to focus on younger children may be too quickly taken as a reason to focus all energy on the younger ages. Indeed, numerous national initiatives have called on communities to focus tremendous energy on the ages from birth to age 3 or from birth to age 5. And, indeed, these are pivotal times in young children's lives, as evidenced, for example, by recent research in brain development during those years.

It is just as important, however, that communities not lose a focus on adolescents—middle and high school youth. As young people move into adolescence, they become increasingly independent from their parents, and they spend more time with peers and in age-specific programming in extracurricular, community, or congregational settings. We sometimes mistake this new independence as a signal that we should stop being engaged in young people's lives. For example, many parents withdraw from involvement in their child's education, structured activities in the community become less common, and adult volunteers are harder to find.

Asset building reminds us that young people continue to need adults in their lives, and they continue to need positive, safe places to spend time, even as they become more autonomous. Indeed, adolescence is a time when young people spend less time with their families and more time in the community with their peers.[7] What do we offer them that will be supportive and enriching, encouraging them to make healthy, positive choices?

[7] R. Larson, "Youth Organizations, Hobbies, and Sports as Developmental Contexts," in R. K. Lilbereisen and E. Todt (Eds.), *Adolescence in Context: The Interplay of Family, School, Peers, and Work in Adjustment.* (New York: Springer-Verlag, 1994).

Signs of Hope ———————————————————

Across the country, hundreds of communities have surveyed local youth to learn about their experiences of assets, the risks and deficits they face, and the behaviors—both positive and negative—in which they engage. And many of these communities have used those data to begin mobilizing to create healthier communities for all their young people. For youth in such communities, a troubled developmental journey may be transformed into a journey filled with promise and possibility.

Youth in these communities will have a greater chance not only of avoiding high-risk behaviors but also of making the most of their talents and interests, both for their own well-being and for the benefit of their communities. In the end, the creative tension that is required in healthy communities—between a positive focus and a problem-centered focus, between informal and formal asset building, between comprehensive and targeted strategies, and all the other tensions we have identified—is not dissimilar from the creative tensions required of successful parents. Successful parents must:

- Balance love and firmness, closeness and independence, membership and individuality;

- Be consistent and repetitious, as well as flexible and able to adapt to their child's changing needs; and

- Provide care and opportunities for children with special needs, as well as opportunities for all their children to grow into the persons they were meant to be.

When a community's neighborhoods, schools, religious institutions, family-serving organizations, youth organizations, and all the other myriad players in young people's lives do the same, then that community is replacing the fragile foundation experienced by too many youth with solid developmental building blocks for all. The challenge is clear; it awaits only our collective will to meet it.

Tapping Deep Cultural Currents

We live in a trend-watching society. Politicians commission public opinion polls. Businesses and investors try to predict or manufacture the next consumer craze. Young people are sharp observers of the latest styles in music and clothing. We are inundated with wave after wave of these up-to-the-minute snapshots of what people think, want, and believe.

But, like the surface waves we see on the ocean, the ever-changing public opinion trends can hide what's going on underneath, where deeper, more powerful currents are shaping the character and future of our society. Those undercurrents may have subtle shifts over time, but the shifts can only be seen in terms of decades and generations, not weeks or even years.

Patterns in the Currents

This report's findings are evidence of deeper currents in our culture—evidence that this nation is failing to pay due attention to the well-being of its children and adolescents. For example:

- Just 4 percent of the young people surveyed meet the standard for well-being we suggest as a target. More young people than this are avoiding risks and deficits. But many of the strengths—assets and thriving indicators—are missing from their lives, interfering with their ability to live optimally.

- Almost two thirds of youth experience fewer than half of the assets. In fact, the average 6th to 12th grader surveyed experiences only 18 of the 40 assets.

- On average, the young people surveyed experience almost two of the five deficits measured.

- Nearly half of those surveyed are engaged in two or more high-risk behavior patterns.

These findings remain fairly consistent in every community studied, regardless of size. Every town, city, and state faces the challenge of having too many young people starting out with a fragile foundation upon which to build their lives. While some youth will certainly beat the odds and do very well, these findings challenge all communities, families, organizations, and individuals to focus energy and commitment on strengthening that foundation.

Undercurrents in the Findings

The major currents or findings, by themselves, do not reflect all the more subtle themes in these data. There are clearly differences in the life experiences of different groups of youth. Some of these differences are evident in these data. A deeper understanding of these differences strengthens our ability to more effectively work with specific groups or individual young people.

In reviewing these differences, it is important to remember that they are, by and large, relatively small. No group of young people is immune from these challenges. And all groups show strengths. In short, the basic, overall messages remain true. The differences point to nuances in the findings.

Age differences

Some of the most notable and consistent differences in the data are based on age. For example, 22 of the assets are at least 10 percentage points lower for 12th graders than for 6th graders. Only three (safety, integrity, and personal power) are that much higher for 12th graders compared to 6th graders. When we compare the grade-by-grade differences, the differences are the greatest during the middle school years, re-emphasizing the importance of responding to the unique developmental needs of young adolescents.

It is impossible to know from these data exactly how to interpret these age trends. Longitudinal research is needed (and under way) that will shed new light. In addition, we need to continue to ask important questions about how to nurture a sense of independence and autonomy while also providing the connections, support, and expectations that guide young people to make healthy choices.

Gender differences

Gender comparisons are another area where we see pervasive, though small, differences (which is consistent with other research in adolescent development).[1] Females are more than twice as likely as males to meet the criteria proposed in Chapter 5 for overall well-being (8 percent vs. 3 percent, respectively). On average, females in this sample experience three more assets than males. Females are also more likely to avoid 4 of the 10 of the high-risk behavior patterns. (The depression or attempted suicide pattern is more common among females, and the differences on the other five indicators are small.)

Furthermore, we find that males are more likely to report only a handful of assets, including self-esteem, safety, and sense of purpose. Females are more likely to report many more of the assets, including service to others, neighborhood boundaries, positive peer influence, creative activities, and all of the internal assets other than the positive identity assets, where levels are roughly the same or males report higher levels, as mentioned above.

These gender differences suggest that a great deal still needs to be learned about the developmental differences and the different contextual experiences of boys and girls. One possibility to explore is whether themes in the assets (connection, caring, self-reflection) are areas of development that are not adequately nurtured and valued in boys and men. We must also continue to examine how society continues to undermine self-esteem and a sense of purpose in girls. And we must find ways to curb violence against women so that young women can be—and feel—safe in their homes, schools, and communities.

In short, we need to understand more fully the unique developmental paths and challenges of both females and males so that we can provide each with appropriate guidance and support in our families, schools, neighborhoods, congregations, youth organizations, and other community settings.

Other differences

Other, less conclusive differences relate to young people from different family compositions or who live in different types of communities (as shown in the appendixes). For example, young people from single-parent families and those who live on reservations tend to have lower levels of assets and higher involvement in high-risk behavior patterns.

It is important, however, not to read too much into these differences, particularly since the present analyses do not control for economic level or poverty. Many of the groups that face greater challenges in some areas (particularly youth from single-parent families, youth who live on reservations, and some youth of color) also face disproportionate levels of poverty, which may explain most, if not all, of the differences observed here. This report does not fully address that question.

All of these differences among various groups of youth, in themselves, point to deep cultural currents. The gender variations highlight differences in the ways boys and girls are socialized. The age differences point to a societal tendency to view mid- and later adolescence as a time of separation and independence without recog-

---

[1] See Nancy Leffert et al., "Developmental Assets: Measurement and Prediction of Risk Behaviors among Adolescents," *Applied Developmental Science, 2* (4), 209-230.

nizing the importance of ongoing connections, relationships, and interdependence as complementary to the development of adult autonomy. And many of the differences among cultural groups, types of communities, and types of families may point to cultural biases, prejudice, and economic injustice.

At the same time, it is important to reiterate that most of the differences among groups are comparatively small and must be viewed in light of the larger context. No group of young people is protected from these challenges, and every group has strengths upon which to build. It is time to move beyond blaming and shaming to finding specific ways to strengthen the developmental foundation for *all* youth.

Deep Cultural Challenges

The overall patterns in this report represent pervasive and perennial currents in this society. *A Fragile Foundation* is being published a decade after Search Institute began measuring assets in youth. Though we can't make direct comparisons to those early studies of the original 30 assets, there is evidence that little has changed. Young people continue to experience only about half of the assets measured. Levels of assets that are measured in the same way in the 30- and 40-asset surveys have remained quite consistent.

So while the community-by-community methodology used to aggregate these data on assets cannot offer irrefutable evidence, the patterns strongly suggest that the findings documented in this report represent more pervasive currents that shape young people's experiences. In short, we are not addressing the fundamental challenges. At least four cultural currents are getting in the way:

1. Isolation of families

The family typically is viewed as the primary agent of socialization. Indeed, the family does have high potential to promote developmental strengths. But even the best of families cannot optimize this development without the active assistance of others. They need ongoing connections and support from their neighborhoods, community organizations, informal networks, and major institutions that reinforce and add to their

strengths. Additionally, family capacity is strengthened when partnerships of family, school, youth organizations, neighborhoods, religious institutions, and other socializing agents unite around a shared commitment and priorities.

An extended exploration of the extent to which this society supports family functioning is beyond the scope of this report. However, there is ample evidence (from trend studies in the United States to cross-national comparisons) that community supports for families are strained or absent. This may be due in part to the following:

- the expectation that the family has sole or dominant responsibility for the care of children;

- patterns of social mobility that cause some families to enter communities without known or easily accessible support systems;

- parents spending more and more hours working; and

- a growing national tendency for adults to disconnect from traditional affiliations and memberships (such as neighborhood associations, civic clubs, and congregations), some of which can provide networks of support.

The framework of developmental assets recognizes the central and unique role that family plays in healthy development. At the same time, it challenges the isolation of families, pointing to the complementary roles of many institutions and individuals in a young person's healthy development. In the process, it invites innovations that break down the isolation of families in ways that both strengthen them and encourage them to reach out to others.

2. Civic disengagement

Building a solid developmental foundation depends largely on consistent, positive adult presence and voice in the lives of children and youth. This needs to extend beyond parents and other family members to include adults in many contexts of young people's lives, including neighborhoods, public gathering places, schools, congregations, youth-serving programs, and places of employment. For such interaction to occur, a community needs societal norms that encourage—even expect—most community residents to connect and engage with each other and with the young people around them.

We are only beginning to gather evidence about what societal norms prevail in this country regarding engagement in the lives of children and adolescents. Early indications suggest that norms favoring disengagement are commonplace. For example:

- The developmental assets that are tied to civic engagement (other adult relationships, community values youth, neighborhood support) are relatively uncommon for the young people we surveyed. For example, only one out of five youth report that their community values youth, and two out of five report that their neighborhood is caring.)

- Research by Public Agenda for the Ad Council has found that, when asked to describe American youth, a majority of adults chose negative descriptors (e.g., undisciplined, disrespectful, unfriendly) as their initial response.[2] These perceptions may make people less likely to get involved with youth.

Too many people have disengaged from public and civic life. Too many have also disengaged from the lives of children and teenagers beyond their own family. Multiple factors may play into this disengagement. One may be the busyness of a fast-paced society that squeezes people's time. One may be a feeling of powerlessness in the face of seemingly overwhelming problems. One may be that many people do not see caring for and connecting with young people as their responsibility. And those who do see this as a responsibility may not know how to act upon that commitment.

Asset building offers a new vehicle for re-engaging the public in community life and in the lives of young people. It reminds people of their responsibilities to all young people and helps them see specific ways they can make a difference in young people's lives. In the process of re-engaging in the lives of children and youth, people reconnect and recommit to their community as well.

3. Professionalization of care

A corollary to civic disengagement is that we have overrelied on professionals to care for the young. In a pointed cultural critique, John McKnight describes the evolution of the American service industry and its unintended consequences. He writes:

> The most significant development transforming America since World War II has been the growth of a powerful service economy and its pervasive serving institutions. Those institutions have ["commoditized"] the care of community and called that substitution a service. As citizens have seen the professionalized service commodity invade their communities, they have grown doubtful of their common capacity to care, and so it is that we have become a careless society, populated by impotent citizens and ineffectual communities dependent on the counterfeit of care called human services.[3]

Intertwined with the social phenomenon of the "commoditization" of care is the dominance of what is often called the deficit-reduction paradigm. In this way of thinking and acting, research and practice are steered to naming, counting, and reducing the incidence of environmental risks (e.g., family violence, poverty, family disintegration) and health-compromising behaviors (e.g., substance use, adolescent pregnancy, interpersonal violence, school dropout). This paradigm, it has been argued, dominates the services and strategies chosen to enhance child and adolescent health. In addition, it has driven resource allocation in federal and foundation initiatives.

Deficit reduction as a way of thinking and mobilization action is not misguided. But, as a dominating paradigm, it may unintentionally strengthen both the overprofessionalization of care and civic disengagement. People feel powerless in the face of overwhelming problems that require professional care. These processes may well be symbiotic. That is, civic disengagement and professionalized forms of addressing child and adolescent health may feed each other.

---

[2] Steve Farkas and Jean Johnson, *Kids These Days: What Americans Really Think about the Next Generation* (New York: Public Agenda, 1997), 8.

[3] John McKnight, *The Careless Society: Community and Its Counterfeit* (New York: Basic Books, 1995), ix-x.

Because of its holistic view of development, the asset framework helps to draw together the pieces of adolescent development in ways that broaden responsibility for young people to include everyone, not just professionals.

4. Lack of socialization consistency

In order to pass on a coherent worldview to children and adolescents, primary socializing systems need to provide consistency in the message. For example, if we strive to develop environmental responsibility, our success is enhanced when family, school, congregation, neighborhood, the media, and others symbolize, articulate, and model this core value.

Consistency used to happen more easily, without as much dialogue or rehearsal because people with similar beliefs lived together in clans, tribes, and small towns. Sometimes, such common beliefs were dysfunctional, as is the case of a shared intolerance for difference. But consistency also matters for transmitting the best in a culture, such as the values of responsibility, compassion, integrity, and justice. Numerous societal trends make consistency more difficult.

- The disconnection of generations from each other has taken from children and youth the daily, ongoing opportunity to learn the wisdom of the ages through relationships with the elders.

- The pervasive influence of many forms of media, which often expose young people to many ways of thinking and choosing, some of which are inconsistent.

- The isolation, competition, and, sometimes, suspicion among the institutions within a community (schools, congregations, service organizations, businesses) that interfere with developing a shared understanding of what's important and how each sector can and does contribute to young people's well-being.

- The growing diversity of this society and our increased exposure to many cultures, worldviews, and beliefs, which—despite many strengths and opportunities this reality brings—also can highlight differences more than commonalities.

To highlight these trends as contributing to inconsistency is not to say that these trends are bad. Indeed, many of these trends are, by and large, positive progress. For example, the increased diversity of the nation has the potential to create greater tolerance, a deeper understanding of the world, and a richer opportunity to learn wisdom from many places, cultures, and traditions. Similarly, age-specific programming and understanding has allowed us to address more completely the specific developmental issues of people throughout the life cycle.

At the same time, even changes that are, by and large, healthy require repatterning our lives to ensure that change does not result in unanticipated negative side effects. Unless, for example, we find ways to encourage greater understanding across cultural, religious, and other differences, those differences can quickly become the focal point for misunderstanding, divisiveness, conflict, and violence.

Socializing consistency must be reclaimed. We need to find new ways to pass along a consistent worldview, shared values, and clear expectations—ways that respect and honor the rich traditions, cultures, and experiences of a pluralistic society. Subgroups, families, and individuals may have additional perspectives on what is good that add richness beyond this common core of values.

It is important to recognize that some differences are profound, even among people of good will. Some values and priorities conflict. For example, we value the freedom of expression guaranteed by the First Amendment, but we also want to protect children from pornography on the Internet. The challenge is to discern a core of values that the vast majority of people can affirm.

In many communities, the framework of assets becomes a helpful starting point for beginning conversations about what we all value for our children and youth. But it is only a starting point. Each community must engage in dialogue to identify a common core of values. That requires building new levels of trust, taking risks, and working through conflict. It also requires articulating and modeling these priorities and values—in all their complexity—for children and adolescents. To do otherwise, via silence or inconsistency, invites confusion and mixed messages.

Emerging Signs of Hope

The framework of developmental assets challenges these cultural trends, suggesting that families cannot build the assets alone, that everyone in a community has both a capacity to make a difference and a responsibility for the well-being of children and youth, that consistent messages are imperative, and that we cannot rely on professionals alone to socialize young people. We must find ways to deepen our knowledge, develop new habits, skills, and norms, and maintain a perspective that pays attention to the waves, but focuses on shifting the deeper currents.

While the patterns we just noted run deep in the culture, we also believe they can change. Other currents give us hope:

1. Deepening knowledge of healthy development

The framework of developmental assets is part of a growing body of knowledge about the building blocks of healthy development. The past 30 years have seen a tremendous increase in understanding of the components of well-being for all ages, including children and adolescents. And while most research, policies, and programs still tend to focus on problems, there is a growing commitment to strength-based approaches to health and well-being.

2. Insights from many cultures

Some of the cultural currents pointed to as challenges are particularly problematic in our Western industrialized society, which places disproportionately high value on productivity, independence, and material wealth. Furthermore, the Information Age, which relies on instant everything, has exacerbated some of these problems, particularly inasmuch as they have severed people from the strengths of their roots.

However, many of the cultures and traditions that are part of the tapestry of this pluralistic society offer wisdom, stories, and strengths that can be retold, renewed, and applied to addressing the deep cultural challenges facing our young people. For example, many communities of color have rich, lasting traditions of intergenerational connections and community—traditions that remain strong in many communities. Many, such as Native Americans, have rituals, traditions, and commitments that make children and future generations a top priority.

These rich traditions have much to teach the dominant culture about being in community and being community for the young. The challenge is to discover ways to share that wisdom and to ensure that it is not lost in the midst of a society shaped by mass media and mass marketing.

3. National concern for children's issues

In some ways, it's high tide for children's issues. Opinion polls show the public seeing children's issues as top priorities for the country. Politicians run on platforms focused on children's issues, education, families, and community strength. And for good reason. A poll by the Coalition for America's Children following the 1996 election found that children's issues ranked high in the minds of voters. "No longer can political observers and pundits declare that children's issues lack political clout," the researchers concluded. "Clearly, surrogates for children—which include adults in most demographic groups—care deeply about children's political fortunes. We now know from this survey that at least two-thirds of every demographic subgroup ranked children's issues an "8" or above on a 10 point scale." [4]

In short, the public is paying attention to children's issues. The challenge is to mobilize people not only to vote with children in mind, but to act with children in mind—to engage personally in the lives and well-being of the young people of their communities.

---

[4] Lake Research/The Tarrance Group, *Great Expectations: How American Voters View Children's Issues* (Washington, D.C.: Coalition for America's Children, 1997), p. ii.

4. Innovations by trailblazers

Another sign of hope is the number of large and small initiatives under way that call Americans to new levels of responsibility for children and adolescents. Hundreds of communities, foundations, corporations, and other organizations are investing time and energy in innovative strategies for building healthy communities and providing opportunities for young people. Individuals and families are committing themselves to new levels of involvement. Young people are finding a voice and adding their perspectives, energy, and creativity to finding solutions.

At the time of this writing, we are aware of about 400 communities that are on the journey of growing asset-rich communities as part of Search Institute's Healthy Communities • Healthy Youth network. These are located from coast to coast, from Alaska to Florida and Maine to California. Most operate at a grassroots level with little direct guidance or support nationally. Each is experimenting, struggling, and discovering—seeking new ways to be healthy communities. In addition, more and more national organizations, statewide networks, and regional groups are exploring their role in supporting asset building.

We do not know how these efforts will ultimately impact young people and the underlying culture. But the energy, spontaneity, and creativity that is present in these and other similar efforts have the potential, in time, of shaping the future in positive ways we have only begun to imagine.

From Innovation to Culture Change

Each of these signs of hope can point us toward new ways to address the cultural challenges that interfere with healthy development. But they are only beginning points. They haven't shifted the dominant cultural currents. If we want to shift the culture, making it more likely that all young people can succeed, we must have the vision, commitment, and stamina to keep these efforts from being little more than surface waves that crest and disappear. The challenge is to build and maintain a deep, lasting momentum and energy that gradually shifts the currents and transforms the culture into one that values, supports, and guides all young people to be all that they can be.

We are just beginning to learn about culture change as it relates to children and adolescents. Much more needs to be learned about how waves of innovation become undercurrents of hope. We must find ways to recognize the signs of progress on the journey without becoming premature in self-congratulations on reaching the destination. In a quick-fix society that looks at quarterly reports for earnings and expects schools to turn around test scores in one year, we need to learn from the wisdom of Native Americans who, when they make decisions, take into account the impact of their choices on the seventh generation of their descendants. Such perspective is sorely absent from most Americans' decision making when it comes to children and adolescents.

The challenge of shifting the currents in society so that they support young people's development is great. But it is not without its rewards. Exiled Burmese activist and 1991 Nobel Peace Prize laureate Aung San Suu Kyi summarizes the opportunity this way:

> To be indifferent to the needs of children is to weaken the foundation of our own future. There are so many children in need all over the world, in need of proper nutrition, in need of adequate shelter and clothing, in need of education, in need of loving care. To help a child build a healthy, joyful life is one of the best contributions we can make toward peace and security in this world.[5]

[5] Quoted in a press release from the International Fellowship of Reconciliation on a September 4, 1997, press conference at the United Nations in which Nobel laureates appealed for a "Decade for a Culture of Nonviolence." (www.gn.apc.org/ifor/decade/oct97.htm)

Background Information and Detailed Findings on Developmental Assets

This appendix presents data on the developmental assets. The tables define each of the 40 developmental assets that we measure (Table A.1) and list the survey question(s) used to assess each asset (Table A.2). Then we have included separate tables showing the percentage of youth reporting each developmental asset by the following demographic variables:

- Race/ethnicity;

- Community size;

- Maternal education; and

- Family composition.

The sample for the data presented here represents an aggregate of 99,462 youth in the 6th to the 12th grade in public and alternative schools from 213 U.S. cities, towns, farms, and reservations who took the *Search Institute Profiles of Student Life: Attitudes and Behaviors* survey during the 1996-97 academic year. As with the sample reported in the body of this report, only those communities that had surveyed at least one grade in grades 6-9 and one from grades 10-12 are included. Although not all communities surveyed the full census of 6th-12th graders, a comparison of schools that surveyed all grades with those that did not revealed only a few minor differences.

A full description of the gender and grade breakdown and self-reported race or ethnicity is given in the body of this report (see Table 1.2).[1] It should be reiterated, however, that the sample was not nationally representative, given that it comprises school districts or communities that have self-selected to administer the survey and that it overrepresents White adolescents who live in smaller cities and towns and whose parents have higher-than-average formal education. Nevertheless, it is a large and somewhat diverse sample and provides a sense of how adolescents in a large number of communities describe their lives. There are many youth who represent different ethnic groups and community sizes, who come from families composed of one parent or two, and who report that their parents have different levels of education. Therefore, while this sample allows some comparisons across these groups, these comparisons should be considered in light of the constraints on generalization posed by the lack of balanced representation of youth of color, youth from urban areas, and youth whose parents have less formal education.

Univariate analyses of variance (ANOVAs) were performed using each of the developmental assets as dependent variables and each of the demographic variables as independent variables in each set of separate ANOVAs. As expected, given the large sample size, main effects were significant. That said, each table that shows the percentage of youth who report the developmental assets by various demographic differences is followed by a table that shows the standardized effect sizes $(d)^2$ comparing each subpopulation to the group of youth from the largest subpopulation represented in our sample. For example, following Table A.3 (which gives the percentage of youth reporting each of the developmental assets by ethnicity), Table A.3A presents the standardized effect sizes comparing each of five groups (i.e., American Indian, Asian American, African American, Hispanic American, and multiracial) to White youth, who represent the largest ethnic group (n = 84,816, or 85%) in our sample.

---

[1] A more detailed discussion of gender and grade differences among adolescents in this sample can be found in Nancy Leffert, Peter L. Benson, Peter C. Scales, Anu R. Sharma, Dyanne R. Drake, and Dale A. Blyth, "Developmental Assets: Measurement and Prediction of Risk Behaviors among Adolescents," *Applied Developmental Science, 2* (1998), 209-230.

The effect sizes shown in each cell of the table allow a better comparison of differences between groups than the observed percentage differences. A judgment can be made of how *meaningful* the percentage differences are, given that a large sample size such as that presented here yields even small differences to be *statistically* significant. However, those statistically significant differences are not necessarily meaningful. As a rule, differences of about .20 are considered small, .50 are moderate, and differences of about .80 are considered large. Generally speaking, differences that are moderate or larger are considered meaningful. Differences that are smaller than .20 are considered negligible.

Each table of standardized effect sizes comparing youth reports of the developmental assets is followed by a discussion of how we understand the differences and what we conclude about them, given that any discussion of what these differences mean must include the caution that any apparent differences, or lack thereof, must be followed with confirmatory research with a more representative sample.

In the tables presented, effect sizes with negative values denote that the developmental asset is reported more frequently by the comparison group, whereas positive values indicate that the group to which the subpopulation is being compared reports the developmental asset more frequently. For example, in column three of Table A.3A, where Asian American youth are compared with White youth, negative values of the effect sizes mean that Asian American youth report the developmental asset more frequently. In contrast, in column five, where Hispanic American youth are compared with White youth, positive values indicate that White youth are reporting the developmental asset more frequently.

---

[2] See J. Cohen, *Statistical Power Analysis for the Behavioral Sciences* (Hillsdale, NJ: Lawrence Erlbaum Associates, 1988).

Definitions of 40 Developmental Assets

EXTERNAL ASSETS		INTERNAL ASSETS	
CATEGORY	**ASSET NAME AND DEFINITION**	**CATEGORY**	**ASSET NAME AND DEFINITION**
Support	1. **Family support**—Family life provides high levels of love and support. 2. **Positive family communication**—Young person and her or his parent(s) communicate positively, and young person is willing to seek advice and counsel from parent(s). 3. **Other adult relationships**—Young person receives support from three or more nonparent adults. 4. **Caring neighborhood**—Young person experiences caring neighbors. 5. **Caring school climate**—School provides a caring, encouraging environment. 6. **Parent involvement in schooling**—Parent(s) are actively involved in helping young person succeed in school.	**Commitment to Learning**	21. **Achievement motivation**—Young person is motivated to do well in school. 22. **School engagement**—Young person is actively engaged in learning. 23. **Homework**—Young person reports doing at least one hour of homework every school day. 24. **Bonding to school**—Young person cares about her or his school. 25. **Reading for pleasure**—Young person reads for pleasure three or more hours per week.
Empowerment	7. **Community values youth**—Young person perceives that adults in the community value youth. 8. **Youth as resources**—Young people are given useful roles in the community. 9. **Service to others**—Young person serves in the community one hour or more per week. 10. **Safety**—Young person feels safe at home, at school, and in the neighborhood.	**Positive Values**	26. **Caring**—Young person places high value on helping other people. 27. **Equality and social justice**—Young person places high value on promoting equality and reducing hunger and poverty. 28. **Integrity**—Young person acts on convictions and stands up for her or his beliefs. 29. **Honesty**—Young person "tells the truth even when it is not easy." 30. **Responsibility**—Young person accepts and takes personal responsibility. 31. **Restraint**—Young person believes it is important not to be sexually active or to use alcohol or other drugs.
Boundaries and Expectations	11. **Family boundaries**—Family has clear rules and consequences and monitors the young person's whereabouts. 12. **School boundaries**—School provides clear rules and consequences. 13. **Neighborhood boundaries**—Neighbors take responsibility for monitoring young people's behavior. 14. **Adult role models**—Parent(s) and other adults model positive, responsible behavior. 15. **Positive peer influence**—Young person's best friends model responsible behavior. 16. **High expectations**—Both parent(s) and teachers encourage the young person to do well.	**Social Competencies**	32. **Planning and decision making**—Young person knows how to plan ahead and make choices. 33. **Interpersonal competence**—Young person has empathy, sensitivity, and friendship skills. 34. **Cultural competence**—Young person has knowledge of and comfort with people of different cultural/racial/ethnic backgrounds. 35. **Resistance skills**—Young person can resist negative peer pressure and dangerous situations. 36. **Peaceful conflict resolution**—Young person seeks to resolve conflict nonviolently.
Constructive Use of Time	17. **Creative activities**—Young person spends three or more hours per week in lessons or practice in music, theater, or other arts. 18. **Youth programs**—Young person spends three or more hours per week in sports, clubs, or organizations at school and/or in the community. 19. **Religious community**—Young person spends one or more hours per week in activities in a religious institution. 20. **Time at home**—Young person is out with friends "with nothing special to do" two or fewer nights per week.	**Positive Identity**	37. **Personal power**—Young person feels he or she has control over "things that happen to me." 38. **Self-esteem**—Young person reports having a high self-esteem. 39. **Sense of purpose**—Young person reports that "my life has a purpose." 40. **Positive view of personal future**—Young person is optimistic about her or his personal future.

Items Used to Measure the 40 Developmental Assets

EXTERNAL ASSETS	QUESTIONS

SUPPORT

1. Family support
- I get along well with my parents.
- My parents give me help and support when I need it.
- My parents often tell me they love me.

2. Positive family communication
- If you had an important concern about drugs, alcohol, sex, or some other serious issue, would you talk to your parent(s) about it?
- I have lots of good conversations with my parents.

3. Other adult relationships
How many adults have you known for two or more years who . . . ?
- Give you lots of encouragement whenever they see you
- You look forward to spending time with
- Talk with you at least once a month

4. Caring neighborhood
- In my neighborhood, there are a lot of people who care about me.

5. Caring school climate
- My teachers really care about me.
- I get a lot of encouragement at my school.
- Students in my school care about me.

6. Parent involvement in schooling
How often does one of your parents . . . ?
- Help you with your schoolwork
- Talk to you about what you are doing in school
- Ask you about homework
- Go to meetings or events at your school

EMPOWERMENT

7. Community values youth
- Adults in my town or city make me feel important.
- Adults in my town or city listen to what I have to say.
- Adults in my town or city don't care about people my age.
- In my town or city, I feel like I matter to people.

8. Youth as resources
- In my family, I feel useful and important.
- I'm given lots of chances to help make my town or city a better place in which to live.
- Students help decide what goes on in my school.

9. Service to others
- During an average week, how many hours do you spend helping other people without getting paid (such as helping out at a hospital, day-care center, food shelf, youth program, community service agency, or doing other things) to make your city a better place for people to live?

10. Safety
How often do you feel afraid of . . . ?
- Walking around your neighborhood
- Getting hurt by someone at your school
- Getting hurt by someone in your home

BOUNDARIES AND EXPECTATIONS

11. Family boundaries
- If I break one of my parents' rules, I usually get punished.
- In my family, there are clear rules about what I can and cannot do.
- How much of the time do your parents ask you where you are going or with whom you will be?

12. School boundaries
- In my school, there are clear rules about what students can and cannot do.
- At my school, everyone knows that you'll get in trouble for using alcohol or other drugs.
- If I break a rule at school, I'm sure to get in trouble.

13. Neighborhood boundaries
- If one of my neighbors saw me do something wrong, he or she would tell one of my parents.

14. Adult role models
- My parents spend a lot of time helping other people.
How many adults have you known for two or more years who . . . ?
- Spend a lot of time helping other people
- Do things that are wrong or dangerous (reversed)

15. Positive peer influence
Among the people you consider to be your closest friends, how many would you say . . . ?
- Drink alcohol once a week or more (reversed)
- Have used drugs such as marijuana or cocaine (reversed)
- Do well in school
- Get into trouble at school (reversed)

16. High expectations
- Teachers at school push me to be the best I can be.
- My parents push me to be the best I can be.

CONSTRUCTIVE USE OF TIME

17. Creative activities
- During an average week, how many hours do you spend practicing or taking lessons in music, art, drama, or dance, after school or on weekends?

18. Youth programs
During an average week, how many hours do you spend . . . ?
- Playing on or helping with sports teams at school or in the community
- In clubs or organizations (other than sports) at school (for example, school newspaper, student government, school plays, language clubs, hobby clubs, drama club, debate)
- In clubs or organizations (other than sports) outside of school (such as 4-H, Scouts, Boys and Girls Clubs, YWCA, YMCA)

19. Religious community
- During an average week, how many hours do you spend going to programs, groups, or services at a church, synagogue, mosque, or other religious or spiritual place?

20. Time at home
- On the average, how many evenings per week do you go out just to be with your friends without anything special to do?

INTERNAL ASSETS	QUESTIONS

COMMITMENT TO LEARNING

21. Achievement motivation
- At school I try as hard as I can to do my best work.
- It bothers me when I don't do something well.
- I don't care how I do in school.

22. School engagement
How often do you . . . ?
- Feel bored at school
- Come to classes without bringing paper or something to write with
- Come to classes without your homework finished
- Come to classes without your books

23. Homework
- On an average school day, about how much time do you spend doing homework outside of school?

24. Bonding to school
- I care about the school I go to.

25. Reading for pleasure
- During an average week, how many hours do you spend reading just for fun (not part of your schoolwork)?

POSITIVE VALUES

26. Caring
How important is each of the following to you in your life?
- Helping other people
- Helping to make the world a better place in which to live
- Giving time or money to make life better for other people

27. Equality and social justice
How important is each of the following to you in your life?
- Helping to reduce hunger and poverty in the world
- Helping to make sure that all people are treated fairly
- Speaking up for equality (everyone should have the same rights and opportunities)

28. Integrity
How important is each of the following to you in your life?
- Doing what I believe is right even if my friends make fun of me
- Standing up for what I believe, even when it's unpopular to do so

29. Honesty
How important to you is telling the truth, even when it's not easy?

30. Responsibility
How important is each of the following to you in your life?
- Accepting responsibility for my actions when I make a mistake or get in trouble
- Doing my best even when I have to do a job I don't like

31. Restraint
- It is against my values to drink alcohol while I am a teenager.
- It is against my values to have sex while I am a teenager.

SOCIAL COMPETENCIES

32. Planning and decision making
Think about the people who know you well. How do you think they would rate you on each of these?
- Thinking through the possible good and bad results of different choices before I make decisions
- Being good at planning ahead

33. Interpersonal competence
Think about the people who know you well. How do you think they would rate you on each of these?
- Caring about other people's feelings
- Feeling really sad when one of my friends is unhappy
- Being good at making and keeping friends

34. Cultural competence
Think about the people who know you well. How do you think they would rate you on each of these?
- Respecting the values and beliefs of people who are of a different race or culture than I am
- Knowing a lot about people of other races
- Enjoying being with people who are of a different race than I am

35. Resistance skills
Think about the people who know you well. How do you think they would rate you on each of these?
- Knowing how to say "no" when someone wants me to do things I know are wrong or dangerous
- Staying away from people who might get me in trouble

36. Peaceful conflict resolution
- Imagine that someone at your school hit you or pushed you for no reason. What would you do?

POSITIVE IDENTITY

37. Personal power
- When things don't go well for me, I am good at finding a way to make things better.
- I have little control over the things that will happen in my life (reversed).

38. Self-esteem
- On the whole, I like myself.
- At times, I think I am no good at all (reversed).
- All in all, I am glad I am me.
- I feel I do not have much to be proud of (reversed).

39. Sense of purpose
- Sometimes I feel like my life has no purpose (reversed).

40. Positive view of personal future
- When I am an adult, I'm sure I will have a good life.

Developmental Assets Reported among 6th- to 12th-Grade Youth, by Race/Ethnicity (in %)

ASSET CATEGORY	ASSET NAME	ALL	AMERICAN INDIAN	ASIAN AMERICAN	AFRICAN AMERICAN	HISPANIC AMERICAN	WHITE AMERICAN	MULTIRACIAL
EXTERNAL								
Support	1. Family support	64	60	55	65	69	64	59
	2. Positive family communication	26	26	23	21	30	26	23
	3. Other adult relationships	41	31	28	39	33	42	38
	4. Caring neighborhood	40	36	24	33	36	41	34
	5. Caring school climate	24	22	25	25	26	24	23
	6. Parent involvement in schooling	29	28	22	35	31	29	28
Empowerment	7. Community values youth	20	18	14	22	19	20	17
	8. Youth as resources	24	24	25	27	24	25	22
	9. Service to other	50	49	48	49	45	50	51
	10. Safety	55	54	49	60	57	55	51
Boundaries and Expectations	11. Family boundaries	43	34	36	45	43	43	43
	12. School boundaries	46	53	52	58	52	45	46
	13. Neighborhood boundaries	46	49	38	46	47	46	43
	14. Adult role models	27	19	27	26	23	28	22
	15. Positive peer influence	60	48	68	57	48	61	49
	16. High expectations	41	42	40	50	47	41	39
Constructive Use of Time	17. Creative activities	19	15	21	18	16	19	21
	18. Youth programs	59	45	50	53	49	60	53
	19. Religious community	64	53	57	67	61	65	56
	20. Time at home	49	45	61	48	49	50	44
INTERNAL								
Commitment to Learning	21. Achievement motivation	63	48	73	63	55	64	57
	22. School engagement	64	47	69	56	54	65	53
	23. Homework	45	42	68	49	45	45	43
	24. Bonding to school	51	44	56	43	49	52	44
	25. Reading for pleasure	24	22	28	23	18	24	30
Positive Values	26. Caring	43	43	55	52	51	42	46
	27. Equality and social justice	45	46	61	62	55	43	52
	28. Integrity	63	55	65	68	64	63	67
	29. Honesty	63	59	66	66	64	63	62
	30. Responsibility	60	55	65	63	65	60	60
	31. Restraint	42	34	53	42	36	43	38
Social Competencies	32. Planning and decision making	29	21	33	28	27	29	24
	33. Interpersonal competence	43	33	42	40	40	44	46
	34. Cultural competence	35	38	55	48	46	33	49
	35. Resistance skills	37	26	41	38	31	38	31
	36. Peaceful conflict resolution	44	27	48	24	27	45	35
Positive Identity	37. Personal power	45	31	35	38	36	47	41
	38. Self-esteem	47	38	39	58	48	47	43
	39. Sense of purpose	55	44	44	57	52	56	47
	40. Positive view of personal future	70	62	68	74	67	71	64

Standardized Effect Sizes *(d)* by Race/Ethnicity*

ASSET	WHITE, AMERICAN INDIAN	WHITE, ASIAN AMERICAN	WHITE, AFRICAN AMERICAN	WHITE, HISPANIC AMERICAN	WHITE, MULTIRACIAL
EXTERNAL					
1. Family support	.10	**.20**	-.01	-.09	-.11
2. Positive family communication	.00	.08	.11	-.09	.06
3. Other adult relationships	**.22**	**.27**	.07	.18	.07
4. Caring neighborhood	.11	**.34**	.16	.09	.15
5. Caring school climate	.05	.02	-.14	-.03	.03
6. Parent involvement in schooling	.03	.16	-.12	-.04	.01
7. Community values youth	.06	.16	-.05	.04	.09
8. Youth as resources	.02	-.17	-.05	.00	.06
9. Service to others	.01	.04	.02	.11	.03
10. Safety	.01	.11	-.10	-.05	.09
11. Family boundaries	.18	.14	-.04	.01	.00
12. School boundaries	-.15	-.14	**-.26**	-.14	-.02
13. Neighborhood boundaries	-.05	.15	.00	-.02	.05
14. Adult role models	**.20**	.00	.04	.10	.13
15. Positive peer influence	**.27**	-.15	.09	**.26**	**.24**
16. High expectations	-.02	.00	-.18	-.13	.03
17. Creative activities	.09	-.06	.03	.08	-.05
18. Youth programs	**.31**	**.21**	.14	**.23**	.14
19. Religious community	**.25**	.18	-.04	.08	.19
20. Time at home	.10	**-.22**	.04	.10	.12
INTERNAL					
21. Achievement motivation	**.33**	-.17	.02	.19	.14
22. School engagement	**.39**	-.09	.19	**.23**	**.25**
23. Homework	.07	**-.47**	-.09	.00	.03
24. Bonding to school	.16	-.09	.18	.05	.16
25. Reading for pleasure	.07	-.09	.04	.16	-.13
26. Caring	-.01	**-.26**	**-.20**	-.17	-.07
27. Equality and social justice	-.05	**-.35**	**-.38**	**-.23**	-.17
28. Integrity	.18	-.04	-.11	-.02	-.07
29. Honesty	.08	-.07	-.07	-.03	.01
30. Responsibility	.11	-.10	-.06	-.11	.01
31. Restraint	.18	**-.20**	.01	.15	.10
32. Planning and decision making	.17	-.10	.02	.04	.11
33. Interpersonal competence	**.21**	.03	.08	.07	-.04
34. Cultural competence	-.11	**-.46**	**-.32**	**-.29**	**-.34**
35. Resistance skills	**.24**	-.07	-.01	.14	.14
36. Peaceful conflict resolution	**.37**	-.06	**.43**	**.38**	**.22**
37. Personal power	**.32**	**.23**	.17	**.21**	.11
38. Self-esteem	.18	.16	**-.22**	-.01	.08
39. Sense of purpose	**.23**	**.22**	-.03	.07	.18
40. Positive view of personal future	.19	.06	-.07	.08	.14

* *d* = (White *M* - Comparison group *M*)/Pooled *SD*. Bold indicates at least small standardized effect sizes.

Race/Ethnicity

In all cases where there are differences between White youth and youth from other ethnic groups, those differences are small ($d = \pm .20$ to $\pm .39$) or negligible ($d < \pm .20$). Several patterns of difference are notable. First, the highest number of small differences between ethnic groups occurs in comparing American Indian adolescents and White American adolescents and in comparing Asian American and White adolescents. American Indian youth report 12 (30%) of the 40 assets less frequently than White youth. There are the same number of differences (12) comparing Asian American youth and White youth. However, 6 of these are reported more frequently by Asian American youth and 6 more frequently by White youth. Again, it should be reiterated that these differences are small, although they occur across 30% of the assets.

Fewer differences are apparent in comparing both African American and Hispanic American adolescents to White adolescents. Five of the six small effects that are observed in comparing African American and White adolescents are in the direction of African American youth reporting the presence of the developmental asset more frequently than White youth. Only one developmental asset (peaceful conflict resolution) is reported more frequently by White youth as compared to African Americans, but that difference, like all the other group differences observed, is small ($d = .43$). Five of the seven differences comparing Hispanic American and White youth are in the direction of White youth reporting the asset more frequently, and two assets (equality and social justice, and cultural competence) are reported more frequently by Hispanic Americans.

The fewest number of ethnic group differences is observed comparing multiracial adolescents and White adolescents; there are four differences that reach a small effect. Three (positive peer influence, school engagement, and peaceful conflict resolution) of these are reported more frequently by White youth; one developmental asset (cultural competence) is reported more frequently by multiracial youth.

Another interesting pattern of difference pertains to *where* the differences seem to be focused (such as what particular categories of assets or differences occur in the external or internal domain). In some of the asset categories there are no differences that even reach a small effect for one or more of the comparisons. For example, there are no differences comparing White youth and any other ethnic group among the empowerment assets. Similarly, although there are some small differences between White adolescents and American Indian and between White and Asian American adolescents in the support assets, there are no differences that even reach a small effect comparing White adolescents with either African American, Hispanic American, or multiracial adolescents. Other such comparisons within a particular category of assets can be seen in Table A.3A.

It is also noteworthy that there are more differences consistently across all of the ethnic group comparisons in the internal asset domain than within the external domain. For example, there is one asset in the external domain (school boundaries) where there is a small difference ($d = -.26$) between African American adolescents and White adolescents. There are five such differences among the assets in the internal domain comparing African American and White adolescents.

Community Size

The largest group of youth in this aggregate sample by community size is made up of those who report that they live in a small city (n = 20,550, or 21% of the sample). As can be seen in Table A.4, there appear to be some percentage differences among youth who live in communities of different sizes. The majority of these differences are negligible. There are four small differences between adolescents from small cities and adolescents who live on farms, with adolescents who live on farms more frequently reporting the presence of the assets compared to adolescents who live in small cities. There is also one difference comparing youth who live in the country to youth who live in small cities: Youth who live in the country report that they spend more time at home than youth from small cities (d = -.32).

However, there are differences in 25 of the assets comparing youth who live on reservations with youth from small cities. Most of these differences are small, but three are of moderate size (achievement motivation = .61, school engagement = .56, and peaceful conflict resolution = .52). As can be seen in Table A.4A, all of the differences are in the direction of youth who live in small cities reporting the asset more frequently than youth who live on reservations.

Developmental Assets Reported among 6th- to 12th-Grade Youth, by Community Size (in %)

ASSET CATEGORY	ASSET NAME*	ALL	FARM	COUNTRY	RESERVATION	SMALL TOWN	TOWN	SMALL CITY	CITY	LARGE CITY
EXTERNAL										
Support	1. Family support	64	61	63	55	63	65	64	66	65
	2. Positive family communication	26	27	27	21	25	26	25	27	27
	3. Other adult relationships	41	44	42	29	39	41	41	41	37
	4. Caring neighborhood	40	50	43	33	40	37	36	37	38
	5. Caring school climate	24	25	24	19	23	25	24	26	27
	6. Parent involvement in schooling	29	27	28	26	29	29	29	31	33
Empowerment	7. Community values youth	20	24	21	16	19	20	18	20	21
	8. Youth as resources	24	26	24	22	22	24	25	27	27
	9. Service to others	50	55	50	46	50	49	48	51	48
	10. Safety	55	60	58	55	57	55	54	49	48
Boundaries and Expectations	11. Family boundaries	43	41	43	28	44	44	43	43	40
	12. School boundaries	46	44	44	42	47	46	44	48	50
	13. Neighborhood boundaries	46	48	46	42	48	46	44	45	43
	14. Adult role models	27	28	27	14	26	27	28	29	25
	15. Positive peer influence	60	63	60	37	57	59	60	62	57
	16. High expectations	41	41	41	38	40	41	41	41	42
Constructive Use of Time	17. Creative activities	19	16	18	16	17	19	20	21	20
	18. Youth programs	59	62	57	51	57	60	60	59	56
	19. Religious community	64	73	64	56	64	64	63	64	58
	20. Time at home	49	68	60	42	47	46	44	42	44
INTERNAL										
Commitment to Learning	21. Achievement motivation	64	61	63	37	61	64	66	68	61
	22. School engagement	64	65	64	39	61	63	65	67	61
	23. Homework	45	43	43	35	43	45	47	52	49
	24. Bonding to school	51	53	50	37	49	51	52	54	51
	25. Reading for pleasure	25	23	26	21	24	25	25	24	22
Positive Values	26. Caring	43	41	42	36	43	44	43	47	49
	27. Equality and social justice	45	40	43	37	45	46	44	48	52
	28. Integrity	64	62	63	48	63	65	64	65	62
	29. Honesty	63	64	64	53	62	63	62	64	63
	30. Responsibility	60	63	61	49	61	61	60	60	59
	31. Restraint	42	43	43	25	40	42	43	46	43
Social Competencies	32. Planning and decision making	29	29	29	18	26	28	30	31	29
	33. Interpersonal competence	44	40	43	27	42	44	44	48	45
	34. Cultural competence	35	26	31	31	34	36	37	40	46
	35. Resistance skills	37	37	37	21	34	37	39	41	37
	36. Peaceful conflict resolution	44	44	43	20	41	44	46	47	40
Positive Identity	37. Personal power	45	44	45	24	43	46	49	47	41
	38. Self-esteem	47	45	46	36	43	46	50	50	48
	39. Sense of purpose	55	55	54	42	52	54	57	57	54
	40. Positive view of personal future	71	68	71	59	68	70	73	73	69

Standardized Effect Sizes *(d)* by Community Size*

ASSET	SMALL CITY, FARM	SMALL CITY, COUNTRY	SMALL CITY, RESERVATION	SMALL CITY, SMALL TOWN	SMALL CITY, TOWN	SMALL CITY, CITY 50-250K	SMALL CITY, LARGE CITY >250K
EXTERNAL							
1. Family support	.06	.02	.19	.02	-.02	-.04	-.02
2. Positive family communication	-.04	-.04	.11	-.00	-.02	-.03	-.04
3. Other adult relationships	-.05	-.01	**.25**	.04	.00	.01	.09
4. Caring neighborhood	**-.27**	-.13	.01	-.08	-.02	-.02	-.04
5. Caring school climate	-.00	-.00	.13	-.03	-.00	-.03	-.05
6. Parent involvement in schooling	.05	.03	.08	.00	.01	-.03	-.09
7. Community values youth	-.14	-.06	.05	-.03	-.03	-.04	-.06
8. Youth as resources	-.03	.02	.07	.05	.02	-.05	-.05
9. Service to others	-.14	-.04	.05	-.03	-.03	-.05	-.00
10. Safety	-.11	-.06	-.02	-.05	-.00	.11	.13
11. Family boundaries	.04	-.00	**.32**	-.00	-.01	.01	.07
12. School boundaries	.00	-.00	.04	-.07	-.03	-.07	-.13
13. Neighborhood boundaries	-.10	-.05	.02	-.10	-.05	-.03	.01
14. Adult role models	-.00	.02	**.31**	.04	.01	-.03	.06
15. Positive peer influence	-.06	.01	**.48**	.07	.02	-.04	.07
16. High expectations	-.02	-.00	.04	.00	-.02	-.01	-.04
17. Creative activities	.10	.05	.10	.08	.03	-.01	.02
18. Youth programs	-.05	.06	.19	.07	.01	.03	.08
19. Religious community	**-.22**	.04	.15	-.02	-.03	-.03	.09
20. Time at home	**-.49**	**-.32**	.02	-.06	-.04	.04	.00
INTERNAL							
21. Achievement motivation	.11	.07	**.61**	.10	.04	-.04	.11
22. School engagement	.00	.03	**.56**	.08	.04	-.05	.09
23. Homework	.07	.07	**.23**	.08	.04	-.10	-.04
24. Bonding to school	-.01	.05	**.30**	.06	.03	-.03	.02
25. Reading for pleasure	.03	-.03	.09	.02	-.01	.02	.06
26. Caring	.03	.02	.13	-.00	-.02	-.08	-.13
27. Equality and social justice	.09	.03	.15	-.02	-.02	-.08	-.14
28. Integrity	.06	.04	**.35**	.03	-.01	-.01	.04
29. Honesty	-.05	-.03	-.19	-.00	-.01	-.03	-.01
30. Responsibility	-.06	-.02	**.21**	-.02	-.02	.00	-.01
31. Restraint	-.00	.01	**.35**	.06	.01	-.01	-.02
32. Planning and decision making	.02	.03	**.26**	.09	.04	-.02	.02
33. Interpersonal competence	.08	.03	**.35**	.03	-.00	-.07	-.02
34. Cultural competence	**.23**	.12	.12	.05	.01	-.07	-.18
35. Resistance skills	.03	.04	**.37**	.09	.04	-.04	.03
36. Peaceful conflict resolution	.03	.06	**.52**	.10	.04	-.03	.12
37. Personal power	.09	.07	**.49**	.12	.05	.03	.14
38. Self-esteem	.08	.07	**.26**	.13	.06	.00	.03
39. Sense of purpose	.04	.06	**.31**	.11	.06	.00	.05
40. Positive view of personal future	.09	.04	**.30**	.10	.05	-.01	.06

*d = (Small city M - Comparison group M)/Pooled SD. Bold indicates at least small standardized effect sizes.

Maternal Education

For the comparisons on maternal education, we collapsed some of the response options on the survey question related to maternal education in order to make more meaningful comparisons. We then compared the group of youth who reported that their mothers either had some college or were college graduates (n = 44,435, or 45% of the sample) with three other groups of youth (i.e., youth who reported that their mothers had a grade school education, some high school or high school graduation, and graduate school education).

As can be seen in Table A.5, there appear to be some percentage differences between youth reports of developmental assets based on maternal education. Only four differences that reach even a small effect are observed in comparing adolescents whose mothers went to college to those adolescents whose mothers went to high school; in all four, youth whose mothers went to college report the asset more frequently (parent involvement in schooling = .22, adult role models = .20,

youth programs = .30, and religious community = .23). There is just one difference between adolescents whose mothers went to college compared to adolescents whose mothers went to graduate school: Adolescents whose mothers went to graduate school report parent involvement in schooling more frequently (d = -.21). In addition, all of the differences noted above are in the external assets.

However, there are differences in reports of 17 of the assets when comparing adolescents whose mothers went to college to the reports of those adolescents whose mothers had a grade school education. All but one of those differences are small (although several approach a moderate effect). There is a moderate effect on reports of personal power (d = .50); 50% of youth whose mothers went to college report personal power compared to 25% of youth whose mothers went to grade school only. It is also noteworthy that there are differences in all four of the assets in the category of positive identity in these comparisons and in four of the five assets in the social-competencies category.

Developmental Assets Reported among 6th- to 12th-Grade Youth, by Maternal Education (in %)

ASSET CATEGORY	ASSET NAME	ALL	GRADE SCHOOL	SOME HIGH SCHOOL	HIGH SCHOOL GRADUATE	SOME COLLEGE	COLLEGE GRADUATE	GRADUATE SCHOOL	DON'T KNOW
EXTERNAL									
Support	1. Family support	64	56	54	60	64	69	72	56
	2. Positive family communication	26	21	19	24	25	29	32	21
	3. Other adult relationships	41	21	31	38	42	46	50	28
	4. Caring neighborhood	40	35	30	38	38	43	46	34
	5. Caring school climate	24	22	19	22	23	28	31	21
	6. Parent involvement in schooling	29	25	18	23	28	34	41	24
Empowerment	7. Community values youth	20	18	14	18	18	23	26	17
	8. Youth as resources	24	27	18	21	23	27	32	21
	9. Service to others	50	48	44	47	49	52	56	47
	10. Safety	55	55	51	55	55	57	55	50
Boundaries and Expectations	11. Family boundaries	43	32	35	41	44	46	47	35
	12. School boundaries	46	47	47	45	43	46	47	51
	13. Neighborhood boundaries	46	46	43	44	44	47	49	45
	14. Adult role models	27	16	15	22	25	33	37	20
	15. Positive peer influence	60	53	44	56	57	65	66	63
	16. High expectations	41	40	36	38	40	43	47	38
Constructive Use of Time	17. Creative activities	19	15	13	15	19	21	27	15
	18. Youth programs	59	45	38	52	61	67	72	44
	19. Religious community	64	56	46	60	65	71	71	56
	20. Time at home	49	54	44	49	48	51	49	53
INTERNAL									
Commitment to Learning	21. Achievement motivation	64	44	52	60	65	69	70	53
	22. School engagement	64	49	53	62	64	68	68	55
	23. Homework	45	41	38	42	45	49	51	41
	24. Bonding to school	51	45	42	49	51	55	56	46
	25. Reading for pleasure	25	18	21	21	25	26	31	22
Positive Values	26. Caring	43	45	43	41	42	45	49	42
	27. Equality and social justice	45	48	47	42	44	45	49	44
	28. Integrity	64	57	61	62	65	65	67	55
	29. Honesty	63	57	60	62	62	65	66	59
	30. Responsibility	60	57	59	60	60	62	62	55
	31. Restraint	42	35	30	38	40	47	49	46
Social Competencies	32. Planning and decision making	29	21	21	27	29	32	35	21
	33. Interpersonal competence	44	33	41	42	44	46	49	35
	34. Cultural competence	35	33	36	32	35	36	42	31
	35. Resistance skills	37	28	27	34	36	41	43	34
	36. Peaceful conflict resolution	44	33	30	40	43	49	49	43
Positive Identity	37. Personal power	45	23	34	43	47	51	51	30
	38. Self-esteem	47	35	36	44	48	52	53	37
	39. Sense of purpose	55	38	42	52	56	60	61	42
	40. Positive view of personal future	71	60	61	69	72	75	75	59

Standardized Effect Sizes *(d)* by Maternal Education*

ASSET	SOME COLLEGE OR COLLEGE, GRADE SCHOOL	SOME COLLEGE OR COLLEGE, SOME HIGH SCHOOL OR HIGH SCHOOL	SOME COLLEGE OR COLLEGE, GRADUATE SCHOOL
EXTERNAL			
1. Family support	**.23**	.17	-.12
2. Positive family communication	.14	.10	-.10
3. Other adult relationships	**.48**	.16	-.11
4. Caring neighborhood	.13	.09	-.10
5. Caring school climate	.09	.11	-.11
6. Parent involvement in schooling	.15	**.22**	**-.21**
7. Community values youth	.07	.09	-.12
8. Youth as resources	-.02	.12	-.14
9. Service to others	.06	.09	-.10
10. Safety	.02	.04	.03
11. Family boundaries	**.27**	.12	-.03
12. School boundaries	**-.48**	.02	-.04
13. Neighborhood boundaries	-.02	.03	-.07
14. Adult role models	**.30**	**.20**	-.16
15. Positive peer influence	.19	.17	-.07
16. High expectations	.05	.08	-.09
17. Creative activities	.14	.15	-.16
18. Youth programs	**.42**	**.30**	-.14
19. Religious community	**.27**	**.23**	-.05
20. Time at home	-.08	.04	.02
INTERNAL			
21. Achievement motivation	**.48**	.17	-.06
22. School engagement	**.38**	.13	-.02
23. Homework	.13	.11	-.08
24. Bonding to school	.17	.12	-.05
25. Reading for pleasure	.17	.11	-.12
26. Caring	-.04	.05	-.10
27. Equality and social justice	-.07	.03	-.09
28. Integrity	.17	.06	-.04
29. Honesty	.13	.04	-.04
30. Responsibility	.09	.02	-.02
31. Restraint	.18	.17	-.09
32. Planning and decision making	**.22**	.11	-.09
33. Interpersonal competence	**.23**	.06	-.08
34. Cultural competence	.05	.06	-.14
35. Resistance skills	**.24**	.03	-.08
36. Peaceful conflict resolution	**.29**	.18	-.05
37. Personal power	**.50**	.16	-.03
38. Self-esteem	**.31**	.16	-.05
39. Sense of purpose	**.41**	.15	-.04
40. Positive view of personal future	**.31**	.14	-.03

*d = (Some college M - Comparison group M)/Pooled SD. Bold indicates at least small standardized effect sizes.

Family Composition

We determined group differences by comparing youth from three types of family structures (live with mother, live with father, live part-time with mother and part-time with father) with youth from two-parent families, which make up the largest group in our aggregate sample ($n = 77,092$, or 78% of the sample). (See Table A.6A.) Only one difference reaches a small effect in the comparison of adolescents who live in a two-parent family and those who live part-time with each of their parents: 66% of adolescents who live with both parents report the asset of school engagement compared to 56% of adolescents who live part-time with each parent ($d = .21$).

Nine of the observed percentage differences comparing adolescents who live with both parents and adolescents who live with their mothers reach a small effect. All of these effects are in the direction of youth from two-parent families reporting the asset more frequently. Adolescents who live in two-parent families are more likely to report a caring neighborhood ($d = .24$), parent involvement in schooling ($d = .21$), family boundaries ($d = .22$), adult role models ($d = .20$), positive peer influence ($d = .26$), involvement in youth programs ($d = .29$) and religious community activities ($d = .35$), reading for pleasure ($d = .36$), and restraint ($d = .24$). As can be seen in Table A.6A, the majority of these differences are in the external asset domain.

There are, however, differences comparing youth from two-parent families with those who live full-time with their fathers in almost half of the assets; these differences are small but fairly pervasive. All of these differences are in the direction of the assets being reported more frequently by youth from two-parent families. For example, five of the six support assets are reported more frequently by youth from two-parent families.

By and large, the differences between groups on the reports of developmental assets based on certain demographic features are small. We have been asked whether the assets "work" for all youth, or even if they reflect things that all young people need. Because we find differences in the assets that are primarily small, it is possible to draw some conclusions regarding the presence of differences, although any conclusions must be followed by further research specifically aimed at a closer examination of these differences.

The ethnic group differences are small and the majority of them lie in the comparisons between White and American Indian youth. It is not possible, given these analyses, to estimate the contribution of poverty, as many American Indian youth are poor. This finding is similar to the comparison between youth living on reservations and those who live in small cities; many young people on reservations are poor, and these analyses do not control for socioeconomic status or poverty. Thus, the differences between White and American Indian youth and the differences between youth living on reservations and those from small cities might disappear if we controlled for these effects.

When we compare maternal education group differences, we observe the same trend: Youth whose mothers have less education are less likely to report the presence of assets in their lives. While this tends to support the hypothesis that poverty could be the significant factor contributing to these observations, further analyses, which are beyond the scope of this appendix, are necessary to explore these connections deeply. It should be kept in mind, however, that the differences, as they are presented here, are mostly small.

It should also be borne in mind that this large sample is not nationally representative. It is therefore possible that potential group differences are being suppressed because the sample, despite various demographic groups represented in it, is more homogeneous than heterogeneous. For example, it is possible that the differences between White youth and other ethnic groups are small because minority groups in this population are more like youth from the majority population than they would be similar to, or are similar to, minority groups from large urban areas.

Developmental Assets Reported among 6th- to 12th-Grade Youth, by Family Composition (in %)

ASSET CATEGORY	ASSET NAME	ALL	LIVE WITH TWO PARENTS	LIVE WITH MOTHER	LIVE WITH FATHER	LIVE PART-TIME WITH EACH PARENT
EXTERNAL						
Support	1. Family support	64	66	59	50	59
	2. Positive family communication	26	27	21	18	24
	3. Other adult relationships	41	43	34	34	38
	4. Caring neighborhood	40	42	31	32	33
	5. Caring school climate	24	26	20	17	23
	6. Parent involvement in schooling	29	31	22	17	27
Empowerment	7. Community values youth	20	21	16	15	17
	8. Youth as resources	25	26	20	19	23
	9. Service to others	50	51	46	41	49
	10. Safety	55	55	53	58	50
Boundaries and Expectations	11. Family boundaries	43	45	35	31	38
	12. School boundaries	46	46	45	42	47
	13. Neighborhood boundaries	46	47	40	38	44
	14. Adult role models	27	29	20	17	21
	15. Positive peer influence	60	62	50	44	55
	16. High expectations	41	42	36	33	40
Constructive Use of Time	17. Creative activities	19	19	16	14	18
	18. Youth programs	59	61	47	45	54
	19. Religious community	64	68	51	45	59
	20. Time at home	50	52	42	41	44
INTERNAL						
Commitment to Learning	21. Achievement motivation	63	65	56	52	58
	22. School engagement	64	66	57	54	56
	23. Homework	45	47	41	36	41
	24. Bonding to school	51	53	45	41	46
	25. Reading for pleasure	24	25	23	20	24
Positive Values	26. Caring	43	44	42	36	42
	27. Equality and social justice	45	45	46	38	44
	28. Integrity	64	64	63	59	59
	29. Honesty	63	64	60	58	59
	30. Responsibility	60	61	58	57	56
	31. Restraint	43	45	33	25	38
Social Competencies	32. Planning and decision making	29	30	25	23	23
	33. Interpersonal competence	43	44	43	36	42
	34. Cultural competence	35	34	39	32	36
	35. Resistance skills	37	39	32	28	32
	36. Peaceful conflict resolution	44	46	37	32	37
Positive Identity	37. Personal power	45	47	40	42	39
	38. Self-esteem	47	48	42	41	42
	39. Sense of purpose	55	57	48	47	48
	40. Positive view of personal future	70	72	65	63	65

Standardized Effect Sizes *(d)* by Family Composition*

ASSET	TWO PARENTS, MOTHER	TWO PARENTS, FATHER	TWO PARENTS, EACH PART-TIME
EXTERNAL			
1. Family support	.14	**.33**	.14
2. Positive family communication	.15	**.22**	.07
3. Other adult relationships	.17	.18	.10
4. Caring neighborhood	**.24**	**.21**	.18
5. Caring school climate	.13	**.20**	.07
6. Parent involvement in schooling	**.21**	**.31**	.09
7. Community values youth	.14	.15	.11
8. Youth as resources	.13	.16	.06
9. Service to others	.10	.19	.05
10. Safety	.06	-.05	.12
11. Family boundaries	**.22**	**.28**	.15
12. School boundaries	.03	.08	.01
13. Neighborhood boundaries	.14	.19	.06
14. Adult role models	**.20**	**.27**	.18
15. Positive peer influence	**.26**	**.39**	.14
16. High expectations	.12	.18	.04
17. Creative activities	.08	.14	.04
18. Youth programs	**.29**	**.35**	.16
19. Religious community	**.35**	**.47**	.19
20. Time at home	.19	**.21**	.15
INTERNAL			
21. Achievement motivation	.19	**.27**	.15
22. School engagement	.17	**.24**	**.21**
23. Homework	.10	**.21**	.11
24. Bonding to school	.16	**.24**	.13
25. Reading for pleasure	**.36**	.11	.01
26. Caring	.03	.17	.05
27. Equality and social justice	.03	.14	.02
28. Integrity	.02	.11	.11
29. Honesty	.08	.13	.01
30. Responsibility	.06	.09	.10
31. Restraint	**.24**	**.41**	.14
32. Planning and decision making	.12	.15	.15
33. Interpersonal competence	.02	.16	.05
34. Cultural competence	-.10	.05	-.04
35. Resistance skills	.15	**.22**	.14
36. Peaceful conflict resolution	.18	**.28**	.19
37. Personal power	.13	.10	.15
38. Self-esteem	.13	.15	.13
39. Sense of purpose	.18	.19	.17
40. Positive view of personal future	.15	**.20**	.15

*d = (Two parents M - Comparison group M)/Pooled SD. Bold indicates at least small standardized effect sizes.

Background Information and Detailed Findings on Developmental Deficits

This appendix presents data on developmental deficits. The tables define each of the developmental deficits that we measure (Table B.1) and list the survey question(s) used to assess each deficit (Table B.2). Then we have included separate tables showing the percentage of youth reporting each developmental deficit by the following demographic variables:

- Race/ethnicity;

- Community size;

- Maternal education; and

- Family composition.

The sample for the data presented here represents an aggregate of 99,462 youth in the 6th to the 12th grade in public and alternative schools from 213 U.S. cities, towns, farms, and reservations who took the *Search Institute Profiles of Student Life: Attitudes and Behaviors* survey during the 1996-97 academic year. As with the sample reported in the body of this report, only those communities that had surveyed at least one grade in grades 6-9 and one from grades 10-12 are included. Although not all communities surveyed the full census of 6th-12th graders, a comparison of schools that surveyed all grades with those that did not revealed only a few minor differences.

A full description of the gender and grade breakdown and self-reported race or ethnicity is given in the body of this report (see Table 1.2).[1] It should be reiterated, however, that the sample was not nationally representative, given that it comprises school districts or communities that have self-selected to administer the survey and that it overrepresents White adolescents who

live in smaller cities and towns and whose parents have higher-than-average formal education. Nevertheless, it is a large and somewhat diverse sample and provides a sense of how adolescents in a large number of communities describe their lives. There are many youth who represent different ethnic groups and community sizes, who come from families composed of one parent or two, and who report that their parents have different levels of education. Therefore, while this sample allows some comparisons across these groups, these comparisons should be considered in light of the constraints on generalization posed by the lack of balanced representation of youth of color, youth from urban areas, and youth whose parents have less formal education.

Univariate analyses of variance (ANOVAs) were performed using each of the developmental deficits as dependent variables and each of the demographic variables as independent variables in each set of separate ANOVAs. As expected, given the large sample size, all main effects were significant. That said, each table that shows the percentage of youth who report the developmental deficits by various demographic differences is followed by a table that shows the standardized effect sizes (d)[2] comparing each subpopulation to the group of youth coming from the largest subpopulation represented in our sample. For example, following Table B.3 (which gives the percentage of youth reporting developmental deficits by ethnicity), Table B.3A presents the standardized effect sizes comparing each of five groups (i.e., American Indian, Asian American, African American, Hispanic American, and multiracial) to White youth, who represent the largest ethnic group ($n = 84,816$, or 85%) in our sample.

---

[1] A more detailed discussion of gender and grade differences among adolescents in this sample can be found in Nancy Leffert, Peter L. Benson, Peter C. Scales, Anu R. Sharma, Dyanne R. Drake, and Dale A. Blyth, "Developmental Assets: Measurement and Prediction of Risk Behaviors among Adolescents," *Applied Developmental Science, 2* (1998), 209-230.

The effect sizes shown in each cell of the table allow a better comparison of differences between groups than either the observed percentage differences or the statistically significant ANOVAs. A judgment can be made of how *meaningful* the percentage differences are, given that a large sample size such as that presented here yields even small differences to be *statistically* significant. However, those statistically significant differences are not necessarily meaningful. As a rule, differences of about .20 are considered small, .50 are moderate, and differences of about .80 are considered large. Generally speaking, differences that are moderate or larger are considered meaningful. Differences that are smaller than .20 are considered negligible.

Each table of standardized effect sizes comparing youth reports of the developmental deficits is followed by a discussion of how we understand the differences and what we conclude about them, given that any dis-cussion of what these differences mean must include the caution that any apparent differences, or lack thereof, must be followed with confirmatory research with a more representative sample. In the tables presented in this appendix, effect sizes with negative values denote that the developmental deficit is reported more frequently by the comparison group, whereas positive values indicate that the group to which the subpopulation is being compared reports the developmental deficit more frequently. For example, in column two of Table B.3A, where American Indian youth are compared with White youth, negative values of the effect sizes mean that American Indian youth report the developmental deficit more frequently. In contrast, in column three, where Asian American youth are compared with White youth, positive values indicate that White youth are reporting the developmental deficit more frequently.

---

[2] See J. Cohen, *Statistical Power Analysis for the Behavioral Sciences* (Hillsdale, NJ: Lawrence Erlbaum Associates, 1988).

Definitions of Developmental Deficits

DEFICIT	DEFINITION
Alone at home	Spends two hours or more per school day alone at home.
TV overexposure	Watches television or videos three or more hours per school day.
Physical abuse	Reports one or more incidents of physical abuse in lifetime.
Victim of violence	Reports being a victim of violence one or more times in the past two years.
Drinking parties	Reports attending one or more parties in the past year "where other kids your age were drinking."

Items Used to Measure Developmental Deficits

DEFICIT	QUESTION
Alone at home	• On an average school day, how many hours do you spend at home with no adult there with you?
TV overexposure	• On an average school day, how many hours do you spend watching TV or videos?
Physical abuse	• Have you ever been physically harmed (that is, where someone caused you to have a scar, black and blue marks, welts, bleeding, or a broken bone) by someone in your family or someone living with you?
Victim of violence	• How many times in the past two years have you been the victim of physical violence where someone caused you physical pain or injury?
Drinking parties	• During the past 12 months, how many times have you been to a party where other kids your age were drinking?

Race/Ethnicity

In most cases, where there are differences between White youth and youth from other ethnic groups, those differences are small ($d = -.20$ to $-.32$) or negligible. Two differences each are notable in comparing African American, Hispanic American, and multiracial youth to White youth. Only one of those differences is moderate in size: 57% of African American adolescents report overexposure to TV compared to 29% of White adolescents ($d = -.63$). More African American youth also report being alone at home, but this differ-ences is small ($d = -.23$). Hispanic American adolescents report more TV overexposure and attendance at parties where drinking takes place than White adolescents, but these differences are also small ($d = -.32$ and $-.26$, respectively). In addition, multiracial youth report a higher incidence of physical abuse and being victims of violence; these differences are small ($d = -.30$ and $-.32$, respectively). All other observed percentage differences between White adolescents and youth from other ethnic groups are negligible.

TABLE B.3

Developmental Deficits Reported among 6th- to 12th-Grade Youth, by Race/Ethnicity (in %)

DEFICIT	ALL	AMERICAN INDIAN	ASIAN AMERICAN	AFRICAN AMERICAN	HISPANIC AMERICAN	WHITE AMERICAN	MULTI-RACIAL
Alone at home	48	51	50	59	49	47	54
TV overexposure	30	39	36	57	43	29	37
Physical abuse	29	35	25	30	28	29	42
Victim of violence	31	38	25	30	28	30	45
Drinking parties	51	55	39	50	64	50	55

TABLE B.3A

Standardized Effect Sizes (d) by Race/Ethnicity*

DEFICIT	WHITE, AMERICAN INDIAN	WHITE, ASIAN AMERICAN	WHITE, AFRICAN AMERICAN	WHITE, HISPANIC AMERICAN	WHITE, MULTIRACIAL
Alone at home	-.08	-.05	**-.23**	-.03	-.12
TV overexposure	**-.24**	-.16	**-.63**	**-.32**	-.19
Physical abuse	-.14	.07	-.03	.02	**-.30**
Victim of violence	-.17	.12	-.01	.04	**-.32**
Drinking parties	-.09	**.22**	.01	**-.26**	-.10

*d = (White M - Comparison group M)/Pooled SD. Bold indicates at least small standardized effect sizes.

Community Size

The majority of youth in this aggregate sample report that they live in a small city (*n* = 20,550, or 21% of the sample). As can be seen in Table B.4, there appear to be some percentage differences in reports of developmental deficits among youth who live in communities of different sizes. All but four of these differences are negligible. There are four differences that reach a small effect size among young people living on reservations compared to adolescents from small cities (Table B.4A) in that adolescents from reservations report four of the five developmental deficits more frequently than adolescents from small cities: TV overexposure (*d* = -.33), physical abuse (*d* = -.20), victim of violence (*d* = -.21), and drinking parties (*d* = -.28). All other observed percentage differences are negligible.

TABLE B.4

Developmental Deficits Reported among 6th- to 12th-Grade Youth, by Community Size (in %)

DEFICIT	ALL	FARM	COUNTRY	RESERVATION	SMALL TOWN	TOWN	SMALL CITY	CITY	LARGE CITY
Alone at home	48	41	44	55	49	49	50	52	54
TV overexposure	30	27	29	44	33	32	29	29	37
Physical abuse	29	30	29	37	30	29	28	28	32
Victim of violence	31	28	30	41	31	31	31	31	34
Drinking parties	51	50	50	67	52	52	53	49	51

TABLE B.4A

Standardized Effect Sizes *(d)* by Community Size*

DEFICIT	SMALL CITY, FARM	SMALL CITY, COUNTRY	SMALL CITY, RESERVATION	SMALL CITY, SMALL TOWN	SMALL CITY, TOWN	SMALL CITY, CITY 50-250K	SMALL CITY, LARGE CITY >250K
Alone at home	.18	.11	-.11	.01	.01	-.04	-.09
TV overexposure	.04	-.01	**-.33**	-.10	-.06	.00	-.18
Physical abuse	-.04	-.03	**-.20**	-.05	-.01	-.01	-.08
Victim of violence	.06	.02	**-.21**	-.01	.01	.01	-.06
Drinking parties	.05	.06	**-.28**	.01	.02	.08	.05

*d = (Small city *M* - Comparison group *M*)/Pooled *SD*. Bold indicates at least small standardized effect sizes.

Maternal Education

For the comparisons on maternal education, we collapsed some of the response options on the survey question related to maternal education in order to make more meaningful comparisons. We then compared the group of youth who reported that their mothers either had some college or had completed college (*n* = 44,435, or 45% of the sample) with three other groups of youth (i.e., youth who reported that their mothers had either a grade school education, some high school or high school graduation, and graduate school education). Of the observed percentage differences shown in Table B.5, only one comparison reaches a small effect: Adolescents who report that their mothers had a grade school education report more TV overexposure than adolescents who report that their mothers had some college or had graduated from college (*d* = -.27). All other percentage differences do not even reach what would be considered a small effect.

TABLE B.5

Developmental Deficits Reported among 6th- to 12th-Grade Youth, by Maternal Education (in %)

DEFICIT	ALL	GRADE SCHOOL	SOME HIGH SCHOOL	HIGH SCHOOL GRADUATE	SOME COLLEGE	COLLEGE GRADUATE	GRADUATE SCHOOL	DON'T KNOW
Alone at home	48	62	68	67	68	68	70	66
TV overexposure	30	58	60	57	55	52	51	63
Physical abuse	29	35	39	30	30	26	28	32
Victim of violence	31	32	38	31	32	28	32	32
Drinking parties	52	52	61	54	56	49	48	36

TABLE B.5A

Standardized Effect Sizes (*d*) by Maternal Education*

DEFICIT	SOME COLLEGE OR COLLEGE, GRADE SCHOOL	SOME COLLEGE OR COLLEGE, SOME HIGH SCHOOL OR HIGH SCHOOL	SOME COLLEGE OR COLLEGE, GRADUATE SCHOOL
Alone at home	-.00	-.02	-.05
TV overexposure	**-.27**	-.13	.02
Physical abuse	-.16	-.08	-.00
Victim of violence	-.05	-.05	-.05
Drinking parties	-.01	-.07	.07

*d = (Some college *M* - Comparison group *M*)/Pooled *SD*. Bold indicates at least small standardized effect sizes.

Family Composition

We determined group differences by comparing youth from three types of family structures (i.e., live with mother, live with father, live part-time with mother and part-time with father) with youth from two-parent families, which make up the largest groups in our aggregate sample (n = 77,092, or 78%). (See Table B.6.) Four out of the five developmental deficits are reported more often by youth living with their fathers compared with those youth from two-parent families, and all four are small effects (d = -.20 to -.36). As can also be seen in Table B.6A, young people who live part-time with each parent also report higher percentages of developmental deficits, with three reaching a small effect (alone at home = -.25, physical abuse = -.22, and victim of violence = -.23). Youth who live with their mothers also report higher percentages of developmental deficits; however, only two out of the five developmental deficits reach a small effect (alone at home = -.30 and drinking parties = -.20). All other percentage differences are negligible.

TABLE B.6

Developmental Deficits Reported among 6th- to 12th-Grade Youth, by Family Composition (in %)

DEFICIT	ALL	LIVE WITH TWO PARENTS	LIVE WITH MOTHER	LIVE WITH FATHER	LIVE PART-TIME WITH EACH PARENT
Alone at home	48	55	60	63	57
TV overexposure	30	29	36	33	32
Physical abuse	29	27	35	36	37
Victim of violence	31	29	37	39	39
Drinking parties	51	49	59	65	52

TABLE B.6A

Standardized Effect Sizes *(d)* by Family Composition*

DEFICIT	TWO PARENTS, MOTHER	TWO PARENTS, FATHER	TWO PARENTS, EACH PART-TIME
Alone at home	-.30	-.36	-.25
TV overexposure	-.14	-.08	-.07
Physical abuse	-.17	-.20	-.22
Victim of violence	-.17	-.23	-.23
Drinking parties	-.20	-.33	-.07

*d = (Two parents M - Comparison group M)/Pooled SD. Bold indicates at least small standardized effect sizes.

Background Information and Detailed Findings on High-Risk Behavior Patterns

This appendix presents data on high-risk behavior patterns. The tables define each of the high-risk behavior patterns that we measure (Table C.1) and list the survey question(s) used to assess each risk pattern (Table C.2). Then we have included separate tables showing the percentage of youth reporting each behavior pattern by the following demographic variables:

- Race/ethnicity;

- Community size;

- Maternal education; and

- Family composition.

The sample for the data presented here represents an aggregate of 99,462 youth in the 6th to the 12th grade in public and alternative schools from 213 U.S. cities, towns, farms, and reservations who took the *Search Institute Profiles of Student Life: Attitudes and Behaviors* survey during the 1996-97 academic year. As with the sample reported in the body of this report, only those communities that had surveyed at least one grade in grades 6-9 and one from grades 10-12 are included. Although not all communities surveyed the full census of 6th-12th graders, a comparison of schools that surveyed all grades with those that did not revealed only a few minor differences.

A full description of the gender and grade breakdown and self-reported race or ethnicity is given in the body of this report (see Table 1.2).[1] It should be reiterated, however, that the sample is not nationally representative, given that it comprises school districts or communities that have self-selected to administer the survey and that it overrepresents White adolescents who live in smaller cities and towns and whose parents have higher-than-average formal education. Nevertheless, it is a large and somewhat diverse sample and provides a sense of how adolescents in a large number of communities describe their lives. There are many youth who represent different ethnic groups and community sizes, who come from families composed of one parent or two, and who report that their parents have different levels of education. Therefore, while this sample allows some comparisons across these groups, these comparisons should be considered in light of the constraints on generalization posed by the lack of balanced representation of youth of color, youth from urban areas, and youth whose parents have less formal education.

Univariate analyses of variance (ANOVAs) were performed using each of the risk patterns as dependent variables and each of the demographic variables as independent variables in each set of separate ANOVAs. As expected, given the large sample size, all main effects were significant. That said, each table that shows the percentage of youth who report engaging in these high-risk behavior patterns by various demographic differences is followed by a table that shows the standardized effect sizes $(d)^2$ comparing each subpopulation to the group of youth coming from the largest such subpopulation represented in our sample. For example, following Table C.3 (which gives the percentage of youth reporting high-risk behavior patterns by ethnicity), Table C.3A presents the standardized effect sizes comparing each of five ethnic groups (i.e., American Indian, Asian American, African American, Hispanic American, and multiracial) to White youth, who represent the largest ethnic group ($n = 84,816$, or 85%) in our sample.

---

[1] A more detailed discussion of gender and grade differences among adolescents in this sample can be found in Nancy Leffert, Peter L. Benson, Peter C. Scales, Anu R. Sharma, Dyanne R. Drake, and Dale A. Blyth, "Developmental Assets: Measurement and Prediction of Risk Behaviors among Adolescents," *Applied Developmental Science, 2* (1998), 209-230.

The effect sizes shown in each cell of the table allow a better comparison of differences between groups than either the observed percentage differences or the statistically significant ANOVAs. A judgment can be made of how *meaningful* the percentage differences are given that a large sample size, such as that presented here, yields even small differences to be *statistically* significant. However, those statistically significant differences are not necessarily meaningful. As a rule, differences of about .20 are considered small, .50 are moderate, and differences of about .80 are considered large. Generally speaking, differences that are moderate in size, or larger, are considered meaningful. Differences that are smaller than .20 are considered negligible.

Each table of standardized effect sizes comparing youth reports of risky behaviors is followed by a discussion of how we understand the differences and what we conclude about them, given that any discus-sion of what these differences mean must include the caution that any apparent differences, or lack thereof, must be followed with confirmatory research with a more representative sample. In the tables presented in this appendix, effect sizes with negative values denote that the risky behavior is reported more frequently by the comparison group, whereas positive values indicate that the group to which the subpopulations is being compared reports the risky behavior more frequently. For example, in column two of Table C.3A, where American Indian youth are compared with White youth, negative values of the effect sizes mean that American Indian youth report the risky behavior more often. In contrast, in column three, where Asian American youth are compared with White youth, positive values indicate that White youth are reporting the risky behavior more frequently.

---

[2] See J. Cohen, *Statistical Power Analysis for the Behavioral Sciences* (Hillsdale, NJ: Lawrence Erlbaum Associates, 1988).

TABLE C.1

Definitions of Patterns of High-Risk Behavior

HIGH-RISK BEHAVIOR PATTERN	DEFINITION
Problem alcohol use	Has used alcohol three or more times in the past 30 days or has gotten drunk once or more in the past two weeks.
Tobacco	Smokes one or more cigarettes every day or frequently uses chewing tobacco.
Illicit drug use	Has used illicit drugs (such as marijuana, cocaine, LSD, PCP or angel dust, heroin or other narcotics, amphetamines) three or more times in the past 12 months.
Sexual intercourse	Has had sexual intercourse three or more times in lifetime.
Depression and suicide	Is frequently depressed and/or has attempted suicide.
Antisocial behavior	Has been involved in three or more incidents of shoplifting, trouble with police, or vandalism in the past 12 months.
Violence	Has engaged in three or more acts of fighting, hitting, injuring a person, carrying or using a weapon, or threatening physical harm in the past 12 months.
School problems	Has skipped school two or more days in the past four weeks and/or has below a C average.
Driving and alcohol	Has driven after drinking or ridden with a drinking driver three or more times in the past 12 months.
Gambling	Has gambled three or more times in the past 12 months.

TABLE C.2

Items Used to Measure High-Risk Behavior Patterns

HIGH-RISK BEHAVIOR PATTERN	QUESTION
Problem alcohol use	• How many times, if any, have you used alcohol to drink during the last 30 days? • Think back over the last two weeks. How many times have you had five or more drinks in a row? (A "drink" is a glass of wine, a bottle or can of beer, a shot glass of liquor, or a mixed drink.)
Tobacco	• During the last two weeks, about how many cigarettes have you smoked? • How many times, if any, in the last 12 months have you used chewing tobacco or snuff?
Illicit drug use	How many times, if any, in the past 12 months have you . . . ? • Used marijuana (grass, pot) or hashish (hash, hash oil) • Used cocaine (crack, coke, snow, rock) • Used heroin (smack, horse, skag) or other narcotics like opium or morphine • Used PCP or angel dust • Used LSD ("acid") • Used amphetamines (for example, uppers, ups, speed, bennies, dexies) without a prescription from a doctor
Sexual intercourse	• Have you ever had sexual intercourse ("gone all the way," "made love")?
Depression and suicide	• How often did you feel sad or depressed during the last month? • Have you ever tried to kill yourself?
Antisocial behavior	During the last 12 months, how many times have you . . . ? • Stolen something from a store • Gotten into trouble with the police • Damaged property just for fun (such as breaking windows, scratching a car, putting paint on walls)
Violence	During the last 12 months, how many times have you . . .? • Hit or beat up someone • Taken part in a fight where a group of your friends fought another group • Hurt someone badly enough to need bandages or a doctor? • Used a knife, gun, or other weapon to get something from a person • Carried a knife or gun to protect yourself • Threatened to physically hurt someone
School problems	• What grades do you earn in school? • During the last four weeks, how many days of school have you missed because you skipped or "ditched"?
Driving and alcohol	During the last 12 months, how many times have you . . . ? • Driven a car after you had been drinking • Ridden in a car whose driver had been drinking
Gambling	• During the last 12 months, how many times have you gambled (for example, bought lottery tickets or tabs, bet money on sports teams or card games)?

Race/Ethnicity

In most cases, where there are differences between White youth and other ethnic groups, those differences are small ($d = \pm .20$ to $\pm .49$). The largest number of differences are observed comparing White and American Indian youth: All of the 10 high-risk behavior patterns are reported more often by American Indian youth, although those differences are, by and large, small or negligible. Only in the case of school problems does the difference reach a moderate effect ($d = -.67$).

Asian American adolescents report lower levels of involvement in all but one risky behavior compared to White youth. However, only two of these reach even a small effect (alcohol; driving and alcohol), and both of those risky behavior patterns are reported more often by White youth. All other observed percentage differences are negligible.

There are four high-risk behavior patterns in which African American youth report the risk behavior more frequently, although those differences are small (i.e., sexual intercourse, antisocial behavior, violence, and school problems). Other risky behavior percentage differences are negligible.

Similar to the differences between American Indian and White youth, Hispanic American and multiracial adolescents report more engagement in risky behaviors than White youth, but these differences are small, except for school problems, in which 37% of Hispanic American youth report having school problems compared to only 18% of White youth, a difference of approximately moderate size ($d = -.49$).

Community Size

The majority of youth in this aggregate sample report that they live in a small city ($n = 20,550$, or 21% of the sample). As can be seen in Table C.4, there appear to be percentage differences among youth who live in communities of different sizes. Almost all of these percentage differences are negligible, except the difference between young people living on reservations compared to adolescents from small cities (Table C.4A). Adolescents from reservations report all 10 of the risky behaviors more often than young people from small cities ($d = -.29$ to $-.80$), with 3 of these being moderate differences (illicit drugs = $-.60$, antisocial behavior = $-.56$, and violence = $-.62$) and a large difference in reports of school problems ($d = -.80$). There is one small difference between youth from farms and youth from small cities, with youth from small cities reporting more illicit drug use than youth who live on farms ($d = .23$).

TABLE C.3

High-Risk Behavior Patterns Reported among 6th- to 12th-Grade Youth, by Race/Ethnicity (in %)

HIGH-RISK BEHAVIOR PATTERNS	ALL	AMERICAN INDIAN	ASIAN AMERICAN	AFRICAN AMERICAN	HISPANIC AMERICAN	WHITE AMERICAN	MULTIRACIAL
Alcohol	27	37	17	22	39	26	32
Tobacco	20	30	13	13	16	19	26
Illicit drugs	18	32	11	22	27	17	28
Sexual intercourse	18	23	12	31	25	17	26
Depression/suicide	23	34	29	28	28	22	35
Antisocial behavior	23	39	21	31	32	22	32
Violence	33	51	28	50	42	31	50
School problems	19	43	16	28	37	18	29
Driving and alcohol	22	32	12	20	32	21	26
Gambling	21	25	18	22	27	20	25

TABLE C.3A

Standardized Effect Sizes (d) by Race/Ethnicity*

HIGH-RISK BEHAVIOR PATTERN	WHITE, AMERICAN INDIAN	WHITE, ASIAN AMERICAN	WHITE, AFRICAN AMERICAN	WHITE, HISPANIC AMERICAN	WHITE, MULTIRACIAL
Alcohol	-.25	.21	.10	-.27	-.12
Tobacco	-.27	.17	.16	.08	-.17
Illicit drugs	-.39	.17	-.12	-.27	-.30
Sexual intercourse	-.16	.13	-.36	-.21	-.22
Depression/suicide	-.29	-.17	-.14	-.16	-.31
Antisocial behavior	-.43	.01	-.22	-.25	-.25
Violence	-.42	.07	-.41	-.24	-.41
School problems	-.67	.05	-.27	-.49	-.30
Driving and alcohol	-.26	.22	.04	-.25	-.13
Gambling	-.11	.06	-.04	-.16	-.11

*d = (White M - Comparison group M)/Pooled SD. Bold indicates at least small standardized effect sizes.

TABLE C.4

High-Risk Behavior Patterns Reported among 6th- to 12th-Grade Youth, by Community Size

HIGH-RISK BEHAVIOR PATTERN	ALL	FARM	COUNTRY	RESERVATION	SMALL TOWN	TOWN	SMALL CITY	CITY	LARGE CITY
Alcohol	27	29	28	46	29	27	26	23	28
Tobacco	20	19	20	34	21	20	19	17	19
Illicit drugs	18	11	17	44	18	19	20	19	23
Sexual intercourse	18	17	17	31	20	20	18	16	21
Depression/suicide	23	20	22	34	26	23	22	22	28
Antisocial behavior	23	19	21	47	24	23	23	22	29
Violence	33	32	33	60	35	33	31	31	40
School problems	19	17	19	48	22	19	17	17	25
Driving and alcohol	22	26	23	38	25	22	20	17	22
Gambling	21	18	20	34	21	21	22	20	23

TABLE C.4A

Standardized Effect Sizes (d) by Community Size*

HIGH-RISK BEHAVIOR PATTERN	SMALL CITY, FARM	SMALL CITY, COUNTRY	SMALL CITY, RESERVATION	SMALL CITY, SMALL TOWN	SMALL CITY, TOWN	SMALL CITY, CITY 50-250K	SMALL CITY, LARGE CITY >250K
Alcohol	-.06	-.03	**-.44**	-.06	-.01	.07	-.05
Tobacco	.02	-.02	**-.35**	-.04	-.01	.07	.00
Illicit drugs	**.23**	.09	**-.60**	.05	.02	.03	-.07
Sexual intercourse	.04	.02	**-.32**	-.04	-.04	.06	-.07
Depression/suicide	.05	-.01	**-.30**	-.10	-.05	-.02	-.15
Antisocial behavior	.11	.05	**-.56**	-.03	.01	.02	-.13
Violence	-.02	-.03	**-.62**	-.08	-.02	.01	-.18
School problems	-.00	-.03	**-.80**	-.12	-.06	-.00	**-.21**
Driving and alcohol	-.15	-.08	**-.45**	-.13	-.06	.06	-.06
Gambling	.10	.06	**-.29**	.03	.03	.04	-.02

*d = (Small city M - Comparison group M)/Pooled SD. Bold indicates at least small standardized effect sizes.

Maternal Education

For the comparisons on maternal education, we collapsed some of the response options on the survey question related to maternal education in order to make more meaningful comparisons. We then compared the group of youth who reported that their mothers either had some college or were college graduates (n = 44,435, or 45% of the sample) with three other groups of youth (i.e., youth who reported that their mothers had a grade school education, some high school or high school graduation, and graduate school education). Adolescents whose mothers had only a grade school education reported that they were more likely to engage in the high-risk behavior patterns compared to youth whose mothers either had some college or were college graduates. On 7 of the 10 high-risk behavior patterns, the percentage differences were small to moderate (d = -.22 to -63). The percentage differences on tobacco use, illicit drugs, and gambling were negligible. The percentage differences are particularly pronounced in reports of school problems, with 39% of youth whose mothers had a grade school education reporting school problems compared with 16% of youth whose mothers either had some college or were college graduates (d = -.63). A small difference also was apparent among youth whose mothers either had some high school or were high school graduates: They report more school problems than youth whose mothers either had some college or had graduated from college (d = -.20).

TABLE C.5

High-Risk Behavior Patterns Reported among 6th- to 12th-Grade Youth, by Maternal Education

HIGH-RISK BEHAVIOR PATTERN	ALL	GRADE SCHOOL	SOME HIGH SCHOOL	HIGH SCHOOL GRADUATE	SOME COLLEGE	COLLEGE GRADUATE	GRADUATE SCHOOL	DON'T KNOW
Alcohol	27	35	38	30	29	23	24	24
Tobacco	20	24	31	23	21	16	15	18
Illicit drugs	18	23	30	19	21	15	16	14
Sexual intercourse	19	27	32	21	20	15	15	14
Depression/suicide	23	34	37	24	23	18	20	29
Antisocial behavior	23	35	35	24	23	19	21	25
Violence	33	49	46	34	33	29	31	38
School problems	19	39	36	21	18	14	14	26
Driving and alcohol	22	30	34	25	23	18	16	20
Gambling	21	23	24	22	22	20	20	18

TABLE C.5A

Standardized Effect Sizes *(d)* by Maternal Education*

HIGH-RISK BEHAVIOR PATTERN	SOME COLLEGE OR COLLEGE, GRADE SCHOOL	SOME COLLEGE OR COLLEGE, SOME HIGH SCHOOL OR HIGH SCHOOL	SOME COLLEGE OR COLLEGE, GRADUATE SCHOOL
Alcohol	**-.22**	**-.13**	.04
Tobacco	**-.18**	**-.16**	.06
Illicit drugs	**-.16**	**-.10**	.03
Sexual intercourse	**-.28**	**-.14**	.05
Depression/suicide	**-.34**	**-.15**	-.00
Antisocial behavior	**-.34**	**-.11**	-.00
Violence	**-.41**	**-.16**	-.02
School problems	**-.63**	**-.20**	.04
Driving and alcohol	**-.23**	**-.15**	.09
Gambling	-.05	-.04	.00

*d = (Some college M - Comparison group M)/Pooled SD. Bold indicates at least small standardized effect sizes.

Family Composition

We determined group differences by comparing youth from three types of family structures (live with mother, live with father, live part-time with mother and part-time with father) with youth from two-parent families, which make up the largest group in our aggregate sample (*n* = 77,092, or 78%). (See Table C.6.) The largest number of differences between youth from different family structures was observed among youth living with their fathers compared to youth in two-parent families. All 10 of the high-risk behavior patterns are reported more often by youth living with their fa-

thers than those from two-parent families (Table C.6), and nine of those are small to almost moderate size (*d* range = -.27 to -.45) (Table C.6A). As can be seen in Table C.6A, young people living only with their mothers also report higher percentages of risky behaviors, with seven being small differences (*d* = -.20 to -.35). Although young people living part-time with either parent also report higher percentages of risky behaviors, only three even reach a small effect (antisocial behavior = -.24, violence = -.27, school problems = -.20); the other seven observed percentage differences are negligible.

TABLE C.6

High-Risk Behavior Patterns Reported among 6th- to 12th-Grade Youth, by Family Composition (in %)

HIGH-RISK BEHAVIOR PATTERN	ALL	LIVE WITH TWO PARENTS	LIVE WITH MOTHER	LIVE WITH FATHER	LIVE PART-TIME WITH EACH PARENT
Alcohol	27	25	33	40	31
Tobacco	19	17	28	34	23
Illicit drugs	18	16	28	32	23
Sexual intercourse	18	16	27	33	19
Depression/suicide	23	21	31	32	29
Antisocial behavior	23	20	31	37	30
Violence	33	31	40	47	43
School problems	19	17	30	34	24
Driving and alcohol	22	20	28	35	27
Gambling	21	20	22	27	24

TABLE C.6A

Standardized Effect Sizes (d) by Family Composition*

HIGH-RISK BEHAVIOR PATTERN	TWO PARENTS, MOTHER	TWO PARENTS, FATHER	TWO PARENTS, EACH PART-TIME
Alcohol	-.19	**-.34**	-.14
Tobacco	**-.28**	**-.44**	-.14
Illicit drugs	**-.31**	**-.43**	-.18
Sexual intercourse	**-.28**	**-.44**	-.07
Depression/suicide	**-.25**	**-.27**	-.19
Antisocial behavior	**-.25**	**-.40**	**-.24**
Violence	**-.20**	**-.36**	**-.27**
School problems	**-.35**	**-.45**	**-.20**
Driving and alcohol	-.19	**-.38**	-.16
Gambling	-.04	-.18	-.10

*d = (Two parents M - Comparison group M)/Pooled SD. Bold indicates at least small standardized effect sizes.

Background Information and Detailed Findings on Thriving Indicators

This appendix presents data on thriving indicators. The tables define each of the thriving behaviors that we measure (Table D.1) and list the survey question(s) used to assess each behavior (Table D.2). Then we have included separate tables showing the percentage of youth reporting each thriving behavior by the following demographic variables:

- Race/ethnicity;

- Community size;

- Maternal education; and

- Family composition.

The sample for the data presented here represents an aggregate of 99,462 youth in the 6th to the 12th grade in public and alternative schools from 213 U.S. cities, towns, farms, and reservations who took the *Search Institute Profiles of Student Life: Attitudes and Behaviors* survey during the 1996-97 academic year. As with the sample reported in the body of this report, only those communities that had surveyed at least one grade in grades 6-9 and one from grades 10-12 are included. Although not all communities surveyed the full census of 6th-12th graders, a comparison of schools that surveyed all grades with those that did not revealed only a few minor differences.

A full description of the gender and grade breakdown and self-reported race or ethnicity is given in the body of this report (see Table 1.2).[1] It should be reiterated, however, that the sample was not nationally representative, given that it comprises school districts or communities that have self-selected to administer the survey and that it overrepresents White adolescents who live in smaller cities and towns and whose parents have higher-than-average formal education. Nevertheless, it is a large and somewhat diverse sample and provides a sense of how adolescents in a large number of communities describe their lives. There are many youth who represent different ethnic groups and community sizes, who come from families composed of one parent or two, and who report that their parents have different levels of education. Therefore, while this sample allows some comparisons across these groups, these comparisons should be considered in light of the constraints on generalization posed by the lack of balanced representation of youth of color, youth from urban areas, and youth whose parents have less formal education.

Univariate analyses of variance (ANOVAs) were performed using each of the thriving indicators as dependent variables and each of the demographic variables as independent variables in each set of separate ANOVAs. As expected, given the large sample size, all main effects were significant. That said, each table that shows the percentage of youth who report the thriving behaviors by various demographic differences is followed by a table that shows the standardized effect sizes $(d)^2$ comparing each subpopulation to the group of youth coming from the largest subpopulation represented in our sample. For example, following Table D.3 (which gives the percentage of youth reporting thriving behaviors by ethnicity), Table D.3A presents the standardized effect sizes comparing each of five groups (i.e., American Indian, Asian American, African American, Hispanic American, and multiracial) to White youth who represent the largest ethnic group ($n = 84,816$, or 85%) in our sample.

---

[1] A more detailed discussion of gender and grade differences among adolescents in this sample can be found in Nancy Leffert, Peter L. Benson, Peter C. Scales, Anu R. Sharma, Dyanne R. Drake, and Dale A. Blyth, "Developmental Assets: Measurement and Prediction of Risk Behaviors among Adolescents," *Applied Developmental Science, 2* (1998), 209-230.

[2] See J. Cohen, *Statistical Power Analysis for the Behavioral Sciences* (Hillsdale, NJ: Lawrence Erlbaum Associates, 1988).

The effect sizes shown in each cell of the table allow a better comparison of differences between groups than either the observed percentage differences or the statistically significant ANOVAs. A judgment can be made of how *meaningful* the percentage differences are, given that a large sample size such as that presented here yields even small differences to be *statistically* significant. However, those statistically significant differences are not necessarily meaningful. As a rule, differences of about .20 are considered small, .50 are moderate, and differences of about .80 are considered large. Generally speaking, differences that are moderate or larger are considered meaningful. Differences that are smaller than .20 are considered negligible.

Each table of standardized effect sizes comparing youth reports of the thriving behaviors is followed by a discussion of how we understand the differences and what we conclude about them, given that any discus-

sion of what these differences mean must include the caution that any apparent differences, or lack thereof, must be followed with confirmatory research with a more representative sample. In the tables presented in this appendix, effect sizes with negative values denote that the thriving indicator is reported more frequently by the comparison group, whereas positive values indicate that the group to which the subpopulation is being compared reports the thriving behavior more frequently. For example, in column three of Table D.3A, where Asian American youth are being compared with White youth, negative values of the effect sizes mean that Asian American youth report the thriving behavior more frequently. In contrast, in column four, where African American youth are compared with White youth, positive values indicate that White youth are reporting the thriving behavior more frequently.

Definitions of Thriving Indicators

INDICATOR	DEFINITION
Succeeds in school	Gets mostly A's on report card.
Helps others	Helps friends or neighbors one or more hours per week.
Values diversity	Places high importance on getting to know people of other racial/ethnic groups.
Maintains good health	Pays attention to healthy nutrition and exercise.
Exhibits leadership	Has been a leader of a group or organization in the past 12 months.
Resists danger	Avoids doing things that are dangerous.
Delays gratification	Saves money for something special rather than spending it all right away.
Overcomes adversity	Does not give up when things get difficult.

TABLE D.2

Items Used to Measure Thriving Indicators

THRIVING INDICATOR	QUESTION
Succeeds in school	• What grades do you earn in school?
Helps others	• During an average week, how many hours do you spend helping friends or neighbors?
Values diversity	• How important to you is getting to know people who are of a different race than you are?
Maintains good health	• Think about the people who know you well. How do you think they would rate you on taking good care of your body (such as eating foods that are good for you, exercising regularly, and eating three good meals a day)?
Exhibits leadership	• During the last 12 months, how many times have you been a leader in a group or organization?
Resists danger	• I like to do exciting things even if they are dangerous.
Delays gratification	• Think about the people who know you well. How do you think they would rate you on saving your money for something special rather than spending it all right away?
Overcomes adversity	• Think about the people who know you well. How do you think they would rate you on giving up when things get hard for you?

Race/Ethnicity

All of the differences between White youth and other ethnic groups in reports of thriving behaviors are small ($d = .21$ to $.39$ and $-.21$ to $-.36$). The largest number of these small differences is observed in comparisons between African American adolescents and White adolescents: There are small differences in four of the eight thriving behaviors. Two of those thriving behaviors (values diversity and resists danger) are reported more often by African American adolescents ($d = -.28$ and $-.41$, respectively), and two of the thriving behaviors (succeeds in school and helps others) are reported more often by White adolescents ($d = .38$ and $.21$, respectively).

Differences in three of the eight thriving behaviors are observed in American Indian and Hispanic American adolescents compared to White adolescents; these differences are also small. The three percentage differences that reach a small effect (succeeds in school, exhibits leadership, and overcomes adversity) among American Indian youth compared with White youth are reported more often by White youth ($d = .39$, $.38$, and $.21$, respectively). Two of the three observed differences between White adolescents and Hispanic American adolescents are reported more often by White adolescents (succeeds in school $= .27$ and exhibits leadership $= .22$). However, 67% of Hispanic American adolescents report that they value diversity compared with 55% of White adolescents ($d = -.25$). There is only one percentage difference on reports of thriving indicators comparing Asian American and White adolescents that reaches a small effect: Asian American youth also report that they value diversity more frequently than White youth ($d = -.36$). There are also two small differences comparing multiracial youth and White youth. White adolescents report more school success than multiracial youth ($d = .26$); multiracial youth are more likely than White youth to value diversity ($d = -.21$). All other ethnic differences on reports of thriving behaviors are negligible.

Thriving Indicators Reported among 6th- to 12th-Grade Youth, by Race/Ethnicity (in %)

THRIVING INDICATOR	ALL	AMERICAN INDIAN	ASIAN AMERICAN	AFRICAN AMERICAN	HISPANIC AMERICAN	WHITE AMERICAN	MULTIRACIAL
Succeeds in school	23	8	29	9	13	25	15
Helps others	83	79	78	76	80	84	83
Values diversity	56	60	73	69	67	55	65
Maintains good health	52	45	54	51	51	52	48
Exhibits leadership	68	56	63	65	58	69	66
Resists danger	20	19	26	36	22	19	16
Delays gratification	46	39	51	43	45	46	41
Overcomes adversity	71	62	63	67	66	72	69

TABLE D.3A

Standardized Effect Sizes (d) by Race/Ethnicity*

THRIVING BEHAVIOR	WHITE, AMERICAN INDIAN	WHITE, ASIAN AMERICAN	WHITE, AFRICAN AMERICAN	WHITE, HISPANIC AMERICAN	WHITE, MULTIRACIAL
Succeeds in school	.39	-.10	.38	.27	.26
Helps others	.15	.17	.21	.11	.04
Values diversity	-.11	-.36	-.28	-.25	-.21
Maintains good health	.14	-.03	.01	.02	.08
Exhibits leadership	.28	.13	.07	.22	.06
Resists danger	.00	-.17	-.41	-.10	.10
Delays gratification	.14	-.09	.07	.01	.10
Overcomes adversity	.21	.18	.11	.13	.05

*d = (White M - Comparison group M)/Pooled SD. Bold indicates at least small standardized effect sizes.

Community Size

The majority of youth in this aggregate sample report that they live in a small city (*n* = 20,550, or 21% of the sample). As can be seen in Table D.4, there appear to be some differences on reports of thriving between youth from different sizes of communities. All but three of those comparisons are negligible. Three of the thriving indicators are reported more often by adolescents who live in small cities compared with the reports of adolescents who live on reservations (succeeds in school = .36, maintains good health = .22, and exhibits leadership = .31).

TABLE D.4

Thriving Indicators Reported among 6th- to 12th-Grade Youth, by Community Size (in %)

THRIVING BEHAVIOR	ALL	FARM	COUNTRY	RESERVATION	SMALL TOWN	TOWN	SMALL CITY	CITY	LARGE CITY
Succeeds in school	24	23	23	11	20	24	27	26	21
Helps others	83	86	85	77	84	83	83	82	79
Values diversity	56	49	53	54	58	59	57	59	64
Maintains good health	52	52	51	42	50	51	52	55	53
Exhibits leadership	68	69	67	56	64	68	71	70	67
Resists danger	20	19	19	16	19	20	19	21	23
Delays gratification	46	51	47	37	44	44	45	46	45
Overcomes adversity	71	73	72	64	69	71	72	71	67

TABLE D.4A

Standardized Effect Sizes (d) by Community Size*

THRIVING BEHAVIOR	SMALL CITY, FARM	SMALL CITY, COUNTRY	SMALL CITY, RESERVATION	SMALL CITY, SMALL TOWN	SMALL CITY, TOWN	SMALL CITY, CITY 50-250K	SMALL CITY, LARGE CITY >250K
Succeeds in school	.08	.08	**.36**	.16	.07	.02	.14
Helps others	-.09	-.05	.16	-.03	-.02	.01	.09
Values diversity	-.16	.08	.06	-.02	-.03	-.05	-.14
Maintains good health	.02	.02	**.22**	.05	.02	-.06	-.01
Exhibits leadership	.03	-.09	**.31**	.15	.06	.02	.09
Resists danger	-.01	.00	.09	.00	.02	-.04	-.09
Delays gratification	-.12	-.05	.16	.01	.02	-.02	-.01
Overcomes adversity	-.01	.00	.18	.06	.02	.01	.12

*d = (Small city *M* - Comparison group *M*)/Pooled *SD*. Bold indicates at least small standardized effect sizes.

Maternal Education

For the comparisons on maternal education, we collapsed some of the response options on the survey question related to maternal education in order to make more meaningful comparisons. We then compared the group of youth who reported that their mothers either had some college or were college graduates (n = 44,435, or 45% of the sample) with three other groups of youth (i.e., youth who reported that their mothers had a grade school education, some high school or high school graduation, and graduate school education). (See Table D.5.) As can be seen in Table D.5A, adolescents whose mothers had only a grade school education reported that they were less likely to exhibit five of the eight thriving behaviors, although these differences are small (d = .22 to .45). Among youth whose mothers had only a grade school education, 9% reported that they succeeded in school compared to 28% of adolescents whose mothers attended college (d = .43). Young people whose mothers attended college are also more likely than those whose mothers attended grade school to report that they help others (d = .22), maintain good health (d = .24), exhibit leadership (d = .45), and overcome adversity (d = .33). Adolescents who report that their mothers went to college are more likely than adolescents whose mothers went to high school to succeed in school (d = .27) and exhibit leadership (d = .24). There were no other meaningful differences between groups comparing level of maternal education.

TABLE D.5

Thriving Indicators Reported among 6th- to 12th-Grade Youth, by Maternal Education (in %)

THRIVING INDICATOR	ALL	GRADE SCHOOL	SOME HIGH SCHOOL	HIGH SCHOOL GRADUATE	SOME COLLEGE	COLLEGE GRADUATE	GRADUATE SCHOOL	DON'T KNOW
Succeeds in school	24	9	9	18	25	31	34	12
Helps others	83	76	81	83	84	85	85	77
Values diversity	56	58	60	55	56	57	60	55
Maintains good health	52	43	41	48	51	57	61	45
Exhibits leadership	68	53	52	64	71	74	77	52
Resists danger	20	22	18	19	18	20	20	22
Delays gratification	46	41	38	44	45	48	50	42
Overcomes adversity	71	59	64	69	73	74	74	62

Standardized Effect Sizes *(d)* by Maternal Education*

THRIVING BEHAVIOR	SOME COLLEGE OR COLLEGE, GRADE SCHOOL	SOME COLLEGE OR COLLEGE, SOME HIGH SCHOOL OR HIGH SCHOOL	SOME COLLEGE OR COLLEGE, GRADUATE SCHOOL
Succeeds in school	**.43**	**.27**	-.13
Helps others	**.22**	.04	-.03
Values diversity	-.04	.01	-.07
Maintains good health	**.24**	.17	-.12
Exhibits leadership	**.45**	**.24**	-.09
Resists danger	-.07	.02	-.02
Delays gratification	.12	.07	-.07
Overcomes adversity	**.33**	.12	-.01

*d = (Some college M - Comparison group M)/Pooled SD. Bold indicates at least small standardized effect sizes.

Family Composition

We determined group differences by comparing adolescents from three types of family structures (live with mother, live with father, live part-time with mother and part-time with father) with adolescents from two-parent families, which make up the largest group in our aggregate sample (n = 77,092, or 78%). (See Table D.6.) There are few meaningful group differences in reports of thriving behaviors, and all differences are small and in the direction of youth from two-parent families reporting higher levels of thriving than youth from the other three groups.

Adolescents who live with two parents report higher levels on three of the eight thriving behaviors than adolescents who live with their fathers. However, these differences are small. Of adolescents who live with their fathers, 11% report that they succeed in school compared to 26% of adolescents from two-parent families (d = .34). More adolescents from two-parent families also report that they maintain good health (d = .21) and exhibit leadership (d = .22) than adolescents who live with their fathers. There is only one difference between adolescents from two-parent families and adolescents who live with their mothers or live part-time with their mothers and part-time with their fathers that reaches a small effect: Adolescents who come from two-parent families are more likely to succeed in school than adolescents who live with their mothers (d = .28) or who live part-time with each parent (d = .21). All other differences between groups based on family structure are negligible.

TABLE D.6

Thriving Indicators Reported among 6th- to 12th-Grade Youth, by Family Composition (in %)

THRIVING INDICATOR	ALL	LIVE WITH TWO PARENTS	LIVE WITH MOTHER	LIVE WITH FATHER	LIVE PART-TIME WITH EACH PARENT
Succeeds in school	23	26	14	11	17
Helps others	83	84	82	79	82
Values diversity	57	56	59	53	58
Maintains good health	52	53	45	43	50
Exhibits leadership	68	69	61	59	65
Resists danger	20	20	19	16	17
Delays gratification	46	47	40	40	43
Overcomes adversity	71	72	67	68	69

Standardized Effect Sizes *(d)* by Family Composition*

THRIVING BEHAVIOR	TWO PARENTS, MOTHER	TWO PARENTS, FATHER	TWO PARENTS, EACH PART-TIME
Succeeds in school	.28	.34	.21
Helps others	.06	.14	.06
Values diversity	-.06	.06	-.03
Maintains good health	.17	.21	.06
Exhibits leadership	.19	.22	.10
Resists danger	.03	.11	.09
Delays gratification	.14	.15	.08
Overcomes adversity	.11	.09	.05

*d = (Two parents M - Comparison group M)/Pooled SD. Bold indicates at least small standardized effect sizes.

Selected Resources

The following asset-building resources (and others) are available from Search Institute, 700 South Third Street, Suite 210, Minneapolis, MN 55415; 800-888-7828; www.search-institute.org

40 Assets: Start Over, Starting Now (Search Institute, 1998). This 8-minute video introduces the 40 assets and shows how individuals and organizations can build them.

101 Asset-Building Actions (Search Institute, 1997). This colorful poster gives ideas for how individuals and institutions can build assets.

All Kids Are Our Kids: What Communities Must Do to Raise Caring and Responsible Children and Adolescents, by Peter L. Benson (Jossey-Bass, 1997). This resource presents the basic vision of asset building and its implications for individual, organizational, and community transformation.

The Asset Approach: Giving Kids What They Need to Succeed (revised), (Search Institute, 1998). This booklet provides a brief, simple introduction to the research and key ideas behind the framework of 40 developmental assets. Available in English or Spanish in packages of 20.

Assets: The Magazine of Ideas for Healthy Communities & Healthy Youth (Search Institute). This quarterly, subscription-based magazine includes stories, ideas, and insights from asset builders across the country.

Building Assets Together: 135 Group Activities for Helping Youth Succeed, by Jolene L. Roehlkepartain (Search Institute, 1998). This book includes hands-on activities and worksheets to use in helping groups of young people explore each of the 40 assets.

Creating Healthy Communities for Kids: Start Over, Starting Now (Search Institute, 1998). This 12-minute video shows how communities across the United States are using the developmental assets to build community for young people.

Profiles of Student Life: Attitudes and Behaviors

The data in this report are aggregated from communities that used Search Institute's survey, *Profiles of Student Life: Attitudes and Behaviors,* to gather information on the assets, risks, thriving indicators, and deficits of their 6th- to 12th-grade youth. For a complete information packet on conducting this survey in your own community, contact Search Institute.

Developmental Assets: A Synthesis of the Scientific Research on Adolescent Development, by Peter C. Scales and Nancy Leffert (Search Institute, 1999). This scholarly book examines more than 800 journal articles and reports that relate to each of the 40 developmental assets, showing the rich heritage that undergirds the asset framework and suggesting additional areas for research.

Healthy Communities • Healthy Youth (revised edition), by Eugene C. Roehlkepartain and Peter L. Benson (Search Institute, 1997). This colorful booklet presents the assets and describes how all individuals and organizations in a community can play an important role in asset building.

Healthy Communities • Healthy Youth Tool Kit (Search Institute, 1998). This binder describes the possibilities for community-wide asset building and offers examples, tips, and tools for addressing 55 different tasks in mobilizing a community.

Pass It On! Ready-to-Use Handouts for Asset Builders (Search Institute, 1999). This collection of reproducible one- and two-page handouts offers asset-building tips for many different people in a community as well as basic information on developmental assets.

Sharing the Asset Message: 40-Asset Speaker's Kit (Search Institute, 1997). This kit includes scripts, color overheads, and reproducible handouts to use in telling others about developmental assets.

Starting Out Right: Developmental Assets for Children, by Nancy Leffert, Peter L. Benson, and Jolene L. Roehlkepartain (Search Institute, 1997). A report that introduces conceptual frameworks of assets for infants and toddlers, preschoolers, and elementary-age children, based on adolescent framework and the literature in child development.

Taking Asset Building Personally (Search Institute, 1999). Developed by Children First, St. Louis Park, Minnesota (the nation's first asset-building initiative), this workbook and leader's guide offer small groups a six-session process for learning about asset building and reflecting on their own asset-building skills and opportunities.

The Troubled Journey: A Portrait of 6th-12th Grade Youth, by Peter L. Benson (Search Institute, 1990, 1993). This research report, originally published in 1990 by Lutheran Brotherhood, first introduced the framework of 30 developmental assets.

You Can Make a Difference for Kids, by Eugene C. Roehlkepartain (Search Institute, 1999). This eight-page booklet introduces the 40 assets and encourages individuals to reflect on their own asset-building experiences and opportunities. It includes tear-out cards that list the 40 assets for four different age-groups: infants and toddlers; preschoolers; elementary-age children; and teenagers.

What Kids Need to Succeed: Proven, Practical Ways to Raise Good Kids (revised edition), by Peter L. Benson, Judy Galbraith, and Pamela Espeland (Free Spirit, 1998). This book includes almost 1,000 ideas for how parents, schools, congregations, youth, and communities can help to build each of the 40 developmental assets.

What Teens Need to Succeed: Proven, Practical Ways to Shape Your Own Future, by Peter L. Benson, Judy Galbraith, and Pamela Espeland (Free Spirit, 1998). This book includes ideas, stories, and tips for teenagers to build assets for themselves and their friends.

What Young Children Need to Succeed: Working Together to Build Assets from Birth to Age 11, by Jolene L. Roehlkepartain and Nancy Leffert (Free Spirit, 1999). This resource offers parents, other adults, and child-serving organizations practical ideas for building assets in infants, toddlers, preschoolers, and elementary-age children.

About the Authors

Peter L. Benson, Ph.D., president of Search Institute, is a social psychologist, author, and speaker who created the original framework of developmental assets and wrote *The Troubled Journey: A Portrait of 6th-12th Grade Youth,* which first introduced the assets in 1990. Dr. Benson has led numerous scientific studies of youth and written dozens of research reports. Among the books he has authored or coauthored are *All Kids Are Our Kids: What Communities Must Do to Raise Caring and Responsible Children and Adolescents* (Jossey-Bass), *What Teens Need to Succeed* (Free Spirit), *What Kids Need to Succeed* (Free Spirit), *Starting Out Right: Developmental Assets for Children* (Search Institute), *Beyond Leaf Raking: Learning to Serve/Serving to Learn* (Abingdon), and *The Quicksilver Years: The Hopes and Fears of Young Adolescents* (Harper & Row).

Peter C. Scales, Ph.D., senior fellow at Search Institute, is widely recognized as one of the nation's foremost authorities on children and families, family life education, and policy development. In addition to numerous scientific articles and chapters, Dr. Scales is author or coauthor of more than a dozen books and monographs, most recently including *Developmental Assets: A Synthesis of the Scientific Research on Adolescent Development* (Search Institute), *Boxed In and Bored: How Middle Schools Continue to Fail Young Adolescents—and What Good Middle Schools Do Right* (Search Institute), and *A Portrait of Young Adolescents in the 1990s* (Search Institute/Center for Early Adolescence), and *Growing Pains: The Making of America's Middle School Teachers* (National Middle School Association).

Nancy Leffert, Ph.D., senior research scientist at Search Institute, is a developmental psychologist, licensed independent clinical social worker, researcher, author, and speaker who specializes in development during adolescence and childhood. She is the 1992 recipient of the Hershel Thornburg Dissertation Award by the Society for Research on Adolescence. Dr. Leffert has previously served in several positions at the University of Minnesota and as director of the Child and Youth Problems Clinic, Family Service Association of San Diego County. In addition to many scientific articles and chapters, Dr. Leffert is coauthor of *Developmental Assets: A Synthesis of the Scientific Research on Adolescent Development, Starting out Right: Developmental Assets for Children, Shema: Listening to Jewish Youth,* and *Making the Case: Measuring the Impact of Youth Development Programs* (all from Search Institute). She earned her doctorate in child psychology from the Institute of Child Development, University of Minnesota, and her master's of social work and bachelor's degree from California State University at San Diego.

Eugene C. Roehlkepartain is director of publishing and communication for Search Institute. Among the books and monographs he has authored or coauthored are *Building Assets in Congregations: A Practical Guide to Helping Youth Grow Up Healthy* (Search Institute), *Learning and Living: How Asset Building Can Unite a School's Mission* (Search Institute), *Parenting with a Purpose: A Positive Approach to Raising Confident, Caring Youth* (Search Institute), *A Practical Guide for Developing Agency/School Partnerships for Service-Learning* (Points of Light Foundation), and *Beyond Leaf Raking: Learning to Serve/Serving to Learn* (Abingdon).

About Search Institute

Search Institute is an independent, nonprofit, nonsectarian organization whose mission is to advance the well-being of adolescents and children by generating knowledge and promoting its application. The institute conducts research and evaluation, develops publications and practical tools, and provides training and technical assistance. It collaborates with others to promote long-term organizational and cultural change that supports the healthy development of all children and adolescents.